Business Owners Speaking from Experience About *No B.S. Ruthless Management of People and Profits*

"Dan gives business owners and managers permission to focus on the mission of growing their business and profits, without the academic wackiness and paternalism that has grown out of the management advice industry. Dan's message may be uncomfortable and not what you want to hear, but he is right on the money. I've been a business owner since 1983 and peaked at 45 employees (now I have 16), and I can tell you that after spending 2 years and $60,000.00 on an MBA, Dan's book is 1,000 times more valuable. If you are ready to re-gain control over your business, this book is for you."

Stephen Oliver, MBA

- President, Mile High Karate® (MileHighKarate.com)
- Franchisor of Martial Arts Schools Nationwide
- CEO, NAPMA: National Association of Professional Martial Artists (NAPMA.com)

"The Professor of Harsh Reality, Dan Kennedy strikes again! Like a red hot poker to the eye, his new book re-defines 'management.' Plain spoken, real world solutions. Insight, clarity and wit. I didn't put this book down until I'd read every word, then called the office and took immediate action on a key employee."

Dave Dickson

- Owner, Ice Cold Air Discount Auto Repair—20 outlets in Florida
- Consultant/coach to owners of auto repair businesses nationwide
- Consultant/coach, all types of businesses—Glazer-Kennedy Insider's Circle Independent Business Advisor, Tampa, Fla. (NoBSTampa.com)

"This book is a 'must read', and more importantly, a 'must implement immediately'—for anyone with employees. Staff is often the Achilles heel in the clinics I manage and those owned by doctors I advise. Utilizing Dan's solid advice has allowed me to successfully manage 55 employees while opening new businesses and achieving record growth in all of them. Each and every book in Dan Kennedy's 'No B.S.' series has commanded my undivided attention, as they should yours."

Chris Tomshak, D.C.

- CEO, HealthSource Inc., national franchisor of chiropractic and weight loss clinics, with over 60 offices

"Dan Kennedy has done it again. He sets the record straight on real life utilization of people and increasing profits."

Ed O'Keefe

- President, DentistProfits.com
- Consultant, coach, marketing systems provider to over 4,000 dental practices

No B.S.

RUTHLESS MANAGEMENT OF PEOPLE & PROFITS

NO HOLDS BARRED
KICK BUTT
TAKE NO PRISONERS
GUIDE TO REALLY
GETTING RICH

Dan Kennedy

EP
Entrepreneur® Press

Jere L. Calmes, Publisher
Cover Design: David Shaw
Production and Composition: Eliot House Productions

Library of Congress Cataloging-in-Publication Data

Kennedy, Dan S., 1954-

No B.S. ruthless management/by Dan Kennedy.

p. cm.—(No B.S. series)

ISBN-13: 978-1-59918-165-3 (alk. paper)

1. Management. 2. Supervision of employees. I. Title. II. Title: No BS ruthless management.

HD31.K4544 2008

658—dc22 2007051574

Printed in Canada

12 11 10 09 08 10 9 8 7 6 5 4 3 2 1

Contents

Preface
Something Different—Straight Talk

I *must begin with a confession:* I *have only one employee* and she is at an office thousands of miles away that I never visit, and we both like it that way. But this happy fact does **not** disqualify me from writing this book. You can relax; I'm not a fuzzy-headed academic, metaphysical softie chock full of personal-growth axioms, ex-coach into team building, or any other sort of theorist. I'm a *very* battle-scarred veteran. I've had as many as 48 employees, had a dozen for a number of years, then 5, then 3, then 1. I've had 'em in manufacturing, retail, direct sales, and publishing businesses. I've employed my parents, my brothers, my wife, my ex-wife, but mostly strangers. MBAs and minimum-wage earners. You will know, when you read this book, that I am "real," that I have been where you are, that I am talking from bloodied-nose experience, not ivory-tower theory.

My clients employ hundreds of thousands of people. I have clients with as many as 1,500 stores, large field sales forces, and, more commonly, 10 to 100 mixed employees—clerical, sales, customer service, fulfillment. At the time that I wrote this, I personally worked, indepth, hands on with owners of 34 different businesses ranging in size from a million dollars or so a year to 30 million. However, through my networks of consultants and coaches, I am in touch with more than 1 million small to medium-sized businesses' owners each year. And one thing they all have in common: gripes, complaints, disappointments, frustrations, pain, and agony with regard to their employees. Much of this has to do with unreasonable expectations and a misunderstanding of the actual nature of employer-employee relationships. Some of it lies squarely at the fault of the business owner for failing in one or more of the Three Requirements for Having Employees: Leadership, Management, Supervision. Some is unavoidable if you must have employees.

I do tell my clients: the fewer, the better—none if possible. I'm much happier without them and you would be, too. And most businesses have many more than they need. But if you insist on having them, they come with Responsibility; there are things you must do continuously to keep them from stealing you blind, to force them to perform to your specifications, to reward those who do, to rid yourself of those who won't. This book is about all those things. For many it will be a bucket of cold water in the face, an eye-opening shocker, a loud, clanging wake-up call. I have been called the Professor of Harsh Reality for a reason. For some, it will be an overdue permission slip to finally start managing your business as if it really is *your* business. For many, it will lead to greater profits, its primary purpose.

This is the sixth book in my *NO B.S.* series. It may be the most No B.S. of them all. Hundreds of thousands of my books have been bought by business owners all over the world, and, fortunately, these readers eagerly await the next title and keep coming back for more. From what they write and tell me, the popularity is thanks to the blunt, unvarnished truth telling, the frank talk, the unequivocal positions. You may not agree with me, but you won't have any confusion about where I stand. These days, that's something. If this is the first No B.S. book you're reading, give it a chance. I think you'll appreciate just how different it is from the other business books you've read. Let me know what you think. You can communicate with me directly, by fax at (602) 269-3113.

—Dan S. Kennedy

PS: There is an important FREE GIFT OFFER from me on page 350 of this book. This Gift can really skyrocket your profits. It's also the way to continue our relationship beyond this book. Please take a minute to act on it.

IMPORTANT NOTICES

1. *The opinions expressed in this book are those of the author, not necessarily those of the publisher.* Some of these opinions are exaggerated in order to make a point, be provocative, or be humorous. The book is intended for people with a sense of humor. One of the author's beliefs is if you don't offend somebody by noon each day, you aren't saying or doing much. He has made sure to exceed quota here. If you are easily offended and do not have a sense of humor, you probably should NOT read this book.

2. *For anyone who is gender or political-correctness sensitive, to head off letters:* The author has predominantly used *he, him,* etc. throughout the book with only occasional exception, rather than awkwardly saying *he or she, him or her*. He does not mean this as a slight to women, only as a convenience. He is not getting paid by the word.
3. *This publication is designed to provide accurate and authoritative information in regard to the subject matter covered.* While every effort has been made to ensure factual accuracy, no warranies concerning such acts are made. This book is published for general information and entertainment purposes only. It is sold with the understanding that the publisher is not engaged in rendering legal, accounting, or other professional services. If legal advice or other expert assistance is required, the services of a competent professional person should be sought.
4. *Employment law is complex and tricky*. This author is not a lawyer or expert in employment law. This book is not intended as legal advice of any kind, including advice regarding employment law. You're on your own. Neither the author nor the publisher accepts any responsibility or liability whatsoever for any decisions you make or actions you take as an alleged result of something you read in this book. Especially if it involves homicide.

Vincent Palko
www.AdToons.com

CHAPTER 1

Gobbledygook "R" Us

"Because of the fluctuational predispositions of your position's productive capacity as juxtaposed to government standards, it would be momentarily injudicious to advocate an increment."
"I don't get it."
"Exactly."

—CONVERSATION BETWEEN ALEXANDER HAIG, THEN SECRETARY OF STATE, AND HIS AIDE

I hold in my hand a brochure sent to me in the mail from a highfalutin university's school of management, attempting to sell me on attending its $4,950.00 two-day seminar titled "Managing the New Workforce: Leadership and Strategy."

This brochure, as well as the seminar it pitches, represents everything that's wrong with at least 90% of everything being fed to business owners and executives about managing people. It is, in a word, b.s.—but let me demonstrate.

First, it's chock full of vague, meaningless gobbledygook. Nice sounding, until you critically analyze it. Here are a few priceless examples:

> **Expand your own perspective and deepen your understanding of how to learn and act on the values and needs that drive a growing portion of your workforce.**

Huh? What, exactly, is the take-away, practical value there? After all, you aren't really interested in running a group therapy program for your employees, are you?

It gets better . . .

> **With demographic shifts come new demands on leaders who must be prepared to find, develop, and retain the New Workforce.**

This is a statement of fact, not a promise of a solution. The brochure is full of these and actually lists only five benefits, one of which is that "expand your own perspective" thing. And, really, what is this "New Workforce" anyway? It's gobbledygook. It makes it sound like aliens from outer space have arrived and suddenly replaced all your employees. Hey, demographic shifts in available employees aren't anything new. They've been a constant since at least the Industrial Revolution. Lincoln freed the slaves. Off we went. Women came into the work force. Asians, Hispanics, MTV-attention-deficit-disordered youth. Pfui. And you don't want to be prepared (with deeper understanding!) to find, develop, and retain any New Workforce anyway. That misses THE point. You want to be prepared to find, develop, and retain a productive work force that produces maximum profit for your business. You see, the professors' very idea of the purpose of employing people, even of owning a company, is misguided. Certainly not in sync with yours.

And I'll bet you'll be wildly excited about this . . .

> **A multigenerational panel discussion will provide an opportunity for participants to interact with undergraduate junior and senior students majoring in business. With an aim toward highlighting both differences and similarities among the generations, participants will come away with a deeper understanding of what makes these young employees tick.**

There sure is a lot of talk here about "deeper understanding." Meaning you, the guy handing out the paychecks, have to more deeply understand the gentle, fragile, difficult-to-motivate, complex individuals entrusted to your care. Gee, sounds like you're running a day-care center.

Now here's what is NOT mentioned anywhere in this brochure: managing people for PROFIT. I read every word very carefully. Since I was occasionally convulsed with laughter, I reread it. The word "profit" does not appear. Not even once.

I wonder why?

Because—like virtually all these university-sponsored seminars, most other management seminars, most management books, most newsletters for managers, and so on—this puppy's being taught by people whose management experience is limited to organizing their sock drawers. No claim is made of even one day spent in the real world, dealing with real employees and real problems—let alone an imperative to create profit. This particular $4,950.00 two-day excursion into the theoretical world of psychobabble has four speakers:

> An Academic Director (whatever that is) who is a visiting lecturer at the school of management. That's it. That's all that's said about her in the brochure. Presumably because there's nothing else to say.

A Chief Marketing Officer and an Adjunct Associate Professor of Marketing at, of course, the school of management. Hmm, Professor of Marketing—maybe he put this nifty brochure together.

A Diversity Coach who wrote a book, *Managing Differently.* Honest to Mabel, a "Diversity Coach!" "Go be diverse for the Gipper!" I wonder, are the Diversity Cheerleaders going to be there too? Maybe a marching band. OK, that's harsh. Heck, I run business coaching programs myself. But this diversity scam has gone way, way too far. It's replaced the sexual harassment and gender sensitivity scam that previously sucked fortunes out of scared corporate coffers. And the fad before it. Enough already. We're diverse. Get over it. Get to work. The *job* isn't diverse. And the *coach* word has become the most overused term since *excellence*.

Nowhere does it say any of these "experts" ever took over a troubled company with horrid employee morale and massive quality control problems and turned it around. Or managed a work force in a way that led to any measurable accomplishment, like increasing profits by 30% over a year. Or even managed a Dairy Queen. It doesn't say any of these things because it's selling *professors*. (If any of them have actually accomplished anything worth bragging about, such as managing a *real* work force, failing to mention it is still telling. It reveals a certain mindset about the relative importance of practical experience and street smarts vs. academic theory and philosophy. There's a smugness to it. The folks with the leather elbow patches on tweed jackets and tenure looking down their noses at us sleeves-rolled-up, boots-in-the-muck folks.)

Of course, YOU are a real business owner in the real world, very unlikely to fall for this. I imagine a bunch of corporate executives who also can't spell *p-r-o-f-i-t* will attend on their companies' tabs and have a grand old time playing eight-people-at-a-table workshop games with their Diversity Coach, then head for happy hour. I doubt you'd catch an entrepreneur in here on a bet.

But the trouble is, this buffoonery and charlatanism seeps out of the colleges' little side businesses and infects the thinking of business owners in many other ways. This sort of academic gobbledygook and classroom theory finds its way into the articles you and I read in real business magazines, into the books on management we might turn to for help. These professor types actually get hired to come in and screw around in real companies we own or invest in or rely on as vendors. They get hired to speak at our associations' conventions. And if you hear this stuff enough, you might think it has a place in your business.

It's actually a cancer on corporate America. Untold millions of dollars and millions of hours are wasted on this sort of thing. Everybody's in meetings and group discussions and quality circles and deeper-understanding retreats when they should be *working*. Managers are embroiled in trying to implement this feel-good, talk-in-circles, meaningless stuff when they need to be *managing*.

I've watched otherwise intelligent CEO's and top executives sit in meetings, listening to this silliness, none willing to state the obvious—that the professor has no clothes—I guess for fear of appearing unsophisticated in front of the others. So budgets get approved by people who won't, themselves, have to suffer through the exercise, who can't clearly explain what they're buying, and who have no way of holding it accountable for increased profits.

It's sad enough this permeates big, dumb companies.

Whatever you do, keep it out of *yours*. You really need to put up barriers. Inoculate yourself. As a good start, any suggestions about managing your business or the people in it coming from somebody who can't show his success at managing businesses (profitably)—like a professor—ought to be ignored or viewed as comedy.

Oh, and to keep picking on the management school's brochure for its seminar, because it's such an easy target: there's one thing other than mention of profit that you won't find anywhere in it—a guarantee. My own company and dozens of my clients often conduct seminars for business owners, with fees ranging from less than $4,950.00 to four times that much. These seminars are always guaranteed, often by more than your money back: if, at the end of the first day, you aren't thrilled with the practical value you're getting, say so, leave, and get a full fee refund plus your airfare and hotel tab reimbursed. Why do *we* do such a thing? Because we can. Why don't the professors? I leave you to your own conclusions. But here are the litmus tests you might consider whenever shelling out your hard-won dough for business advice:

1. It's from somebody who's been where you are and done what you hope to do.
2. It's from somebody with real business battle scars.
3. It's from somebody who can prove profit comes from his advice—preferably in his own past or present businesses as well as others'.
4. It comes with a guarantee.

Diversity Company Non-Fight Song

With new awareness we worship the gods of
Diversity, Sensitivity, and Flexibility
And cheerfully pretend Kwanza is
a real holiday.
Go D-I-V-E-R-S-I-T-E-E!

No Christmas trees, no Easter candy
But time off with pay to fight global warming
is fine 'n' dandy.
Go D-I-V-E-R-S-I-T-E-E!

At this company men can look pretty,
oh so pretty
cuz we have classes in
sexual orientation sensitivity.
Go D-I-V-E-R-S-I-T-E-E!

For the new youth we must take special care
never to upset their delicate disposition
Criticism or be-back-from-lunch-on-time . . . beware
hostile workplace litigation
Go D-I-V-E-R-S-I-T-E-E!

Diversity Company Non-Fight Song

If he wears his backward hat indoors or
brings his goat to work
your new managerial imperative is to overlook.
Respect his unique cultural dignity.
Practice flexibility!
Go D-I-V-E-R-S-I-T-E-E!

Demanding uniformity
stifles their creativity;
at the assembly line
it's the new hate crime.
Go D-I-V-E-R-S-I-T-E-E!

Clearly the new management think works so well
with all the cars we make recalled,
with customer service exported to India.
You may think you died and went to business hell
and wonder why truth and common sense so mauled,
but you just need to be more Mahatma Gandhia!
Go D-I-V-E-R-S-I-T-E-E!

Performance standards show no sensitivity.
Productivity is culturally subjective.
Tough-minded management, not a feasibility.
Only a Neanderthal would make profit the objective.
Go D-I-V-E-R-S-I-T-E-E!

CHAPTER 2

The True Nature of the Employer-Employee Relationship

One friend in a lifetime is much; two are many; three are hardly possible.

—HENRY ADAMS

Few people ever want to acknowledge that the relationship between employer and employees is inherently *adversarial.*

It is adversarial because your agenda is in conflict with theirs, and you are constantly interfering with their ability to act out their agenda. To impose your agenda, you must displace or disrupt their agenda. Bluntly, you are a giant pain the ass.

Here's what might surprise you: I am *not* suggesting there's something wrong with this, or that the employees are bad people for having 13 or 30 or 300 things on their minds ranking in higher priority, interest, and importance to them than the one thing on top of your mind. I do not fault them at all for having their agenda. To expect otherwise is simply stupid.

FIGURE 2.1: Conflicting Agendas

ON THEIR MINDS	ON YOURS
1. Taking care of kids 2. Holding marriage together 3. Planning for upcoming vacation, holiday, etc. 4. Planning for upcoming weekend 5. Planning night out with the girls/guys 6. Getting bills paid 7. Grocery shopping 8. Finding out who Sue slept with over the weekend/office gossip 9. Who will win *American Idol*? 10. Social relationships at the office; who's a bitch, who's my friend 11. Social activities at the office: lunch, football pool, birthdays 12. Getting to work on time 13. Getting off work right on time or early if possible 14. Compliance with "The Program" 15. How much profit can I produce for the company today?	1. How much profit can we produce today?

"Ownership Mentality" Is B.S.

They do not own your business. You do. Expecting employees to have "ownership mentality" is bull crap, despite the idea's popularity with some management gurus. It's irrational. It's like trying to make the zebras on display at Disney's Animal Kingdom® park care deeply and profoundly about how many tickets were sold at the front gate today! The zebras care about getting enough good food to eat and not being eaten by a bigger animal. You can put 'em in team building retreats all you want; they're still coming back with eating as #1, not being eaten as #2, finding warm sun to lie in #3, and it's a long, long way down their list before ticket sales comes up.

Your business is your life and your life is your business. They are intertwined and inseparable. Not so for your employees. Shocking as it may be to you, they have lives all their own. They think about all sorts of things a lot that you barely think about at all, like the price of gas or lettuce or movie tickets. They think *TGIF.* You think: *I need another day this week to work.* They hope no customers wander in 15 minutes before closing time to delay their escape; you pray somebody comes in. You care passionately about profit. They probably don't think about it at all, or, if they do, they resent how much of it you make at their expense, through their sweat and blood.

You own the zoo. They are zebras.

Their agendas are often at opposition with yours, as in the previous example: They want to hurry customers out 15 minutes before closing whether they buy anything or not, so they can get out the door a minute early to meet their friends over at Applebee's® before the chicken wings get cold. You want every customer treated like fragile china, made to feel welcome, courteously helped, never rushed and sold something, even if your employee has to close 15 minutes late. You are not on the same page here and never will be. Not even with employees paid commissions or bonuses. I have been hurried out of an OfficeMax store 15 minutes before closing, but I've also been rushed out of a car dealership at 3:00 P.M. on a Sunday afternoon. At home their spouse, whom they sleep with and, depending on how long married, occasionally have sex with, and who therefore has more clout than you do, is leaning on them to be home or at the restaurant or at Johnny's T-ball game ON TIME. Angry if they aren't. And, of course, completely disinterested in your agenda.

On top of all that, there is the unavoidable resentment that comes with disparities in wealth and power. Consequently, if you could be privy to their discussions behind your back or among friends and family, you would hear that resentment bubble up and expressed constantly, many different ways, and agreed with and encouraged by those around them. I've even sat forgotten in clients' waiting rooms or small offices near enough to the front desk to eavesdrop, and heard these conversations taking place on the employer's time. Frequently, I've sat in the first row in first class and listened to the pilots and stewardesses having these conversations. Your employees tend to believe they are doing all the work and you are getting all the money, and they count gross, not net. They see your new car, hear of you redecorating your house, see you away from the store at your beach house while they toil in the hot sun in the fields, and they resent you for it. The very fact that you can fire them but they can't fire you, that you dictate when they can take a vacation but you take yours whenever you feel like it, pisses them off. They think they are smarter than you are, know better than you do, and they resent having to go along with your crazy schemes and new ideas.

No B.S. Ruthless Management Truth #1

Employees are employees.

They are *not* your friends. You can and, to a degree, should be friendly with them and encourage them to be friendly with you. You want whatever foxhole camaraderie can be created as you go. Just don't lose sight that if you're trapped together in the foxhole when all the food runs out, they won't hesitate to carve you up for dinner. Of course you should recognize their birthdays, childbirths, and anniversaries and genuinely care about their health and well-being. Just know that the birthday cake they bring in for you has arrived only partly because of friendship but partly because of obligation and compulsion.

They are *not* your family. You can be familial to a degree if you like. But don't con yourself. They will not be visiting you at the assisted living center after the paychecks stop. They have a family and you aren't in it.

They are your employees.

The Requirement of "Accurate Thinking"

In the book *Think and Grow Rich,* Napoleon Hill presented 17 principles practiced by the hundreds of great industrialists and entrepreneurs of his time. The one least interesting to the book's millions of readers is Accurate Thinking. Everybody likes the Desire one, but nobody seems to like the Accurate Thinking one. They like the pleasant ones. But Hill didn't mean the 17 as a cafeteria, any more than Moses meant to report the Ten Suggestions as a mix 'n' match, pick 'n' choose menu. On Hill's list, it's my opinion the least liked Accurate Thinking is the most important. If you refuse to think about your real relationship with your employees accurately, rationally, and realistically, you are forever doomed to disappointment, frustration, rage, and financial losses throughout your business. If you acknowledge the true relationship and think about it accurately, you will manage your business and the people in it very differently than if you insist on thinking of these people as friends, family, team members, or even colleagues.

Recommended Resource #1

Napoleon Hill is best known for his book *Think and Grow Rich*, and I recommend reading or re-reading what he has to say in it about accurate thinking. I also strongly recommend his last and least famous book, *Grow Rich with Peace of Mind*.

On TV, I think on the Discovery Channel, I saw this report about a guy who went into the woods to live with bears. He believed the bears had intelligence and souls and were caring individuals. He projected onto them human characteristics, just like we do to our pets, and just like we project onto our employees the characteristics we want them to have. He grew his hair, made himself smell like bears, and actually did move into a cave with a big family of bears. He made this into the relationship with the bears that he wanted to have with them. This was my dad's downfall in his brief experience in sales management, in network marketing: he had a very different relationship with his distributors in his mind than existed in reality. One day, with no apparent provocation, the bears ate this guy. His family and the people making the documentary were properly horrified, and much moaning and hand-wringing went on. *Why oh why would the bears do such a thing?*

Because they are bears.

And wild bears' relationship with dull-witted, foolish, and slow humans is: they're food.

The only sensible question is: Why did the bears wait so long to eat him?

"BUT DAN, WHO WILL SIGN ALL OUR PAYCHECKS?"

Vincent Palko
www.AdToons.com

CHAPTER 3

Shelby's Excuse List

I had thought very carefully about committing hari-kari (ritual suicide) over this, but I overslept this morning.

—FORMER JAPANESE LABOR MINISTER TOSHIO YAMAGUCHI

For several years, I had an interest in a small chain of cosmetic salons. We were not required to have licensed cosmeticians because our employees only talked the customers through the process of applying their own glop. They were really salespeople in lab coats, primarily selling a nonsurgical face-lift kit, then selling for about $300.00. The biggest of the salons, and the one where the weekly batch of new hires came to work their first couple of weeks, was in our office building, just down the hall from my office. With my door open, I could hear our rather coarse sales manager, a guy named Shelby, yelling every morning: "Just give me the damn number!"

On the wall in Shelby's office, there was a large poster board with a numbered list of excuses for being late for work. #14: *My dog swallowed my car keys. #37: It's my time of month. #41: I got on the wrong bus.* He said it saved a lot of time just having them tell him the appropriate number.

This was comedy at the time. I thought Shelby was funny, the situation funny, actually the whole business funny.

But it's also symbolic of something that's not funny at all: accepting unacceptable behavior.

My friend and speaking colleague Zig Ziglar tells an old story about how a frog can get cooked in the squat. Since a frog has the ability to jump quite high, if you take a frog and toss him in a big pot of boiling water, he'll jump right out. But if you put the frog in a pan of room temperature water, he'll stay there. Frogs like water. Then if you ever so slowly turn up the heat on the stovetop he may sit there still, not really noticing the water getting warmer and warmer and warmer until—in spite of his God-given ability to save himself—he gets cooked in the squat.

This is how a lot of business owners get cooked in the squat by their employees. The employees' behavior worsens gradually over time. Little by little by little, one bad one poisons the others. Occasional tardiness becomes frequent tardiness, then constant tardiness. Sloppy appearance goes from rare to occasional to routine. Work left undone, rare, occasional, common. And the business gets cooked in the squat.

If you occasionally accept occasional unacceptable behavior, it's only a matter of time before you'll be routinely accepting routine unacceptable behavior.

Vincent Palko
www.AdToons.com

CHAPTER 4

The Willy Loman Syndrome Moves to Management

I have 14 other grandchildren and if I pay one penny now, then I'll have 14 kidnapped grandchildren.

—J. PAUL GETTY, EXPLAINING HIS REFUSAL TO PAY A RANSOM

Willy Loman is the lead character in Arthur Miller's play *Death of a Salesman*. The death of a salesman is a desperate desire to be liked, above all else—including making sales. This is so common a disease among failing sales professionals, it's called the Willy Loman Syndrome. However, it is contagious beyond salespeople. Managers get infected, too. A manager is severely handicapped, dangerously vulnerable, and certain to be ineffective if he is an approval seeker, a person who needs to be *liked* by his subordinates.

Why the word *ruthless* in this book's title? Isn't that a bit harsh? Most business owners are anything but. They give chance after chance after chance, tolerate incompetence and insubordination, twist themselves into a pretzel trying not to fire even the worst employee ever to walk the earth. Most business owners try too hard to be "a good boss," meaning a boss liked by the employees, rather than an effective boss, or one who sets and enforces standards and procedures in order to create maximum possible profits. I find even ex-Marine tough guys who are pretty ruthless in other aspects of their business soft as mashed potatoes when it comes to managing the people they pay. Many enunciate fear statements, like "If I demand she does that, she'll quit" or wimp statements like "My people just won't do that." Even though in my consulting and coaching relationships, I'm supposed to be dealing with marketing, I find myself fixing these travesties, helping business owners grow a pair. So I think *ruthless* is the direction most need to move in.

One of my favorite stories from the trenches involves the owner of a company with 22 offices scattered over three states and a corporate office really running three businesses in one. After about three years of working with me, his longtime executive assistant came out and told him: "You were a much nicer guy before you started listening to that Kennedy guy," and "I don't like working here anymore." Notably, his company's profits had increased nearly 35% over those three years. He correctly suggested to her it would be most appropriate for her to find a different place of employment where she could be happier. As an accountant, he was able to grasp the fact that there's no bonus added by the bank to his deposits nor extra contribution made to his retirement fund because Bertha was *happy*. Of course I'm not advocating intentionally making everybody unhappy. But somehow, employees and opinion makers have gotten it into their heads that it's your job to make your employees happy. They forget you are paying them to work and generate profits. There are businesses that make people happy, ranging from Disneyland® to Nevada brothels. They all charge fees *for* doing so.

So, yes, I very deliberately used the word *ruthless* to grab attention. One person's *ruthless* is another person's *sane* approach to business. After you read this book, you can draw your own conclusions.

I expect some very harsh, critical reviews. I expect about 33% of the business owners to recoil from what I've put between these pages as they might if finding a bevy of large snakes busily consuming rats under the bedsheets. If that's you, I offer no apologies. Only sympathy. I will probably hear from some of you. It won't be fan mail. You might want to know before writing that I practice as policy "immunity to criticism."

I expect about 33% to rejoice that—*finally*—somebody is speaking the truth and providing both permission to behave in a sane manner as a business owner toward employees and honestly practical advice for doing so. I expect to hear from a lot of you. Of your relief. Of being emboldened. Of your success.

I expect the middle 33% to just be perplexed. But then, the middle 33% is pretty much perplexed 100% of the time about 100% of everything. You know who they are, in your company and out on the street. Easy to spot. They have that perplexed look on their faces.

If you're in the 33% who are rejoicing, congratulations and welcome.

What you need to know most is that Willy Loman would be even more of a failure as a manager than he was as a salesman. There is absolutely no evidence whatsoever that a manager liked by the employees creates more productivity or more profitability for the company. In fact, in sports it's rather common to see underperforming players rallying around the unsuccessful coach they like, trying to keep him from being fired. Not only is the boss who's liked by everybody not any more successful than the boss who's not liked at all, but he may even be less successful. It's OK and probably advisable to take "being liked" off the table altogether. There are a number of other, more important priorities.

CHAPTER 5

The Program

I believe in benevolent dictatorships, provided I am the dictator.

—Richard Branson

A lot of business owners get the performance from their employees they deserve because they have no real Program. As in "Hey, what's the Program around here?" You've asked it when you have first reported to a new job at a new place. So does everybody else.

The Program is the way things are supposed to be done.

If you don't have a Program, you can't very well expect anybody to follow your Program, can you?

I'm not talking about the deadly dull, from a boilerplate template, with legal gobbledygook employee manual. I'm talking about clearly stated, illustrated, and taught expectations for how

Bill and Betty are supposed to talk, walk, act, do. If you don't have a Program, your employees make up their own. They tell the new guy what their Program is. If you leave people to their own devices, you leave your outcomes to chance.

CHAPTER 6

The Two Most Crucial Management Decisions of All

I do not like broccoli and I haven't liked it since I was a little kid. I am President of the United States and I am not going to eat it anymore."

—President George H. W. Bush

A crucial management decision is: What kind of employee do you want? When I ask that question of individual clients or groups of people, I usually get a litany of vague and nice-sounding responses. *I want productive employees. Employees that care. Loyal. Ambitious. Intelligent. With good communication skills. With good attitudes.*

This is akin to, when asked to define goals, answering with "I want to be happy." Not a target. Just an idea.

The only rational answer to this critically important question is: "I want a PROFITABLE employee."

Contrary to a lot of silly ideas, the only sane reason to have an employee is profit. Somehow you get more profit by having the employee than by not having the employee. The only reason to have an employee is that you make a multiple of what he costs by having him. Unfortunately, a lot of people pile up employees around them for remarkably irrational reasons!

In addition to all the management stuff to be discussed in this book, meeting this goal requires four other things: (1) buying into the premise; (2) calculating true and total cost; (3) creating a means of measurement for return on investment (ROI); and (4) vicious intolerance for unsatisfactory ROI.

The Premise

Liberals, most Democrats, some Republicans, Lou Dobbs at CNN, and most employees think you, the business owner, exist to provide people with jobs. This is bullshit. If you can make more money by employing fewer people, that is exactly what you ought to do. In fact, it is your responsibility to do so, because your first and foremost responsibility as CEO is to maximize company income and shareholder value. If you own the thing, then you are CEO *and* shareholder. You have a responsibility to yourself to maximize profit. Only you are invested, only you are at risk, only you truly care. If you go belly up, they'll go get jobs someplace else. It is not your responsibility to provide Mary with a job, nor is it your responsibility to pay her enough to support herself, her uneducated and refusing-to-get-educated husband, three kids, dog, two cars, five cell phones, cable TV with premium channels. It is Mary's responsibility to make herself so valuable your business can't live without her. It is Mary's responsibility to continue making herself more and more valuable so you keep paying her more and more. If she doesn't, if she's an interchangeable commodity, so be it. **It's really important for you to get clear about who owns which responsibilities.** Mary might never get clear about this. Lou Dobbs might never get clear about this. But at least you can get clear about it. A lot of business owners get bullied into having and keeping unprofitable employees because those employees need their jobs. It seems incredible but it's true. This sense of obligation or this guilt over doing so well yourself must be resisted with all your might.

The *only* reason to have or keep Mary around is profit.

The Other Reasons NOT *to Have Employees*

Other unforgivable reasons that business owners have employees, more employees than they need and unprofitable employees, are ego, poor self-esteem, and a need for reassurance, social activity, and friends. Some equate success with having a bigger staff than the next guy. When the brother-in-law who's the doctor visits, the business owner doesn't feel good about showing him a 600-square-foot hole in the wall with one employee at a desk counting money—no matter how much money he's counting. The business owner wants to show his brother-in-law, the doctor, a big beehive of activity with worker bees buzzing about, flying hither and yon. Other business owners lack confidence in their decision making and need a bunch of people around who are paid to agree with them. Other owners can't stand working alone and need to populate a place with people. Instead, I recommend getting a dog. The only reason to have or keep an employee is profit. (There are lots of good reasons to have a dog. If you are unfamiliar with them, read *Marley and*

Me, quite possibly the best book ever written by anybody about anything, period.)

It is your role to keep wage costs to the lowest possible number. With that said, I do believe in Chapter 23's title, "Exceptions to All the Rules." I also believe in suppressing wages for ordinary people who deliver only ordinary performance or people in mundane jobs with inherently low value by any and all legal means necessary so that you, the owner, take home as much money as possible from your business. As I was writing this, by the way, much noise was being made about the U.S. wages for bottom-rung jobs in service sectors like hotels and restaurants actually declining in recent years. According to Lou Dobbs, this is a direct result of the invasion of illegal immigrants who work for less, thus suppressing wages for everybody. And he may be right about this. Personally, I favor locking down our borders for many reasons other than the possibility of wage suppression for people in bottom-of-the-ladder jobs. Here's why: A lot of these jobs are not inherently worth even our minimum wage, so as far as I'm concerned, any force that adjusts the wage down to the real value of the work being done is okeydokey by me. Second,

NO B.S. Ruthless Management Truth #2

Take home as much money as you can from *your* business. No nickel left behind.

and more importantly, it is not any employer's responsibility to pay more than he must or more than a job is worth. It is the responsibility of the person doing that job and dissatisfied with its wage to somehow move up the ladder to more important and therefore better-paying jobs.

Incidentally, there's a ton of b.s. spread around about money, including the idea that rich business owners are NOT working people. A few facts. The number of U.S. penta-millionaires (worth upwards of $5 million) has more than quadrupled in the last ten years, to more than 930,000. The people in that group are mostly entrepreneurs. None got there by working in secure jobs at the post office, the department of motor vehicles, or some big corporation. Only 10% of their wealth comes from inheritance, and only 10% from passive investments; 80% comes from *earned* income. Meaning they worked for it. Quite patiently too, as most made their fortune in a big lump, after many years of effort, sacrifice, and risk. Most employees work 40-hour weeks; most business owners work 60- to 70-hour weeks. Should *anybody* want much greater income and financial security, there is a known, clear, present, and rather formulaic path to getting it.

In a speech in Cleveland on July 4, 2007, Presidential candidate John Edwards flatly stated: "No one in America should work at a full-time job and still be in poverty." This is bullshit piled high and stinking strong. It ignores the fact that lots of folks put themselves in poverty and keep themselves in poverty by birthing multiple children they can't afford to care for; by engaging in money-wasting habits they can't afford, including smoking, drinking, and gambling; and most of all by refusing to move themselves up from a lowest-paying job to a better job and again to a better job. It focuses only on societal, government, and marketplace responsibility but not at all on personal responsibility. It ignores the fact that merely raising wages is inflationary and encourages downsizing, job exporting, and automation, thereby making things worse, not better, for the lowest-skilled workers earning the lowest wages. It is shamefully disingenuous or horribly ignorant or some of each. Having said that, I happen to agree that in a country as rich as ours is—especially rich in opportunity—it is a crying shame that anyone willing to work remain in poverty. But the answers will never be found in the government forcibly raising wages. It's much more complex than that. And it has to start with truth telling in place of pandering. I believe I have a lot more honest compassion for the working poor than Edwards and his ilk, because I would tell them the truth instead of perpetually waving the utterly false hope in front of them that somebody else—Edwards, Hillary, Lou Dobbs—is going to ride in on a white horse and lift them up out of poverty.

We desperately need to tell everybody the blunt truth about this. We need to say: You *shouldn't* make a good living wage to support your family by cleaning the toilets and sweeping the floors at the local motel. That job was never designed or intended to be your career. You should use it only as a step to the next step to the next step. And you should step as fast as you can—like somebody stepping from stone to stone, crossing a swamp. You should haul ass over to the library at night or go on the internet or find a friend to advise you or save up money and take classes to acquire additional, more valuable skills. You should beg your employer for a chance to step up and use those better skills for better income or move on to a different employer who offers a better ladder of opportunity. Maybe you should start a part-time, homebased business on the side and work toward the day you can be in business for yourself. But you shouldn't stay put in a low-value, low-wage job and somehow expect employers or the government or Lou Dobbs to increase your wages again and again. We need to educate people that getting a certain job done has only so much value, and that value does not increase by the number of years a person does it or by the person's need for income. We need to admit that our safety nets are severely flawed and porous and aren't likely to improve much, so you don't want to be dependent on them . . . but that our country offers enormous, varied, accessible opportunities, so you'd better pick one and get in gear. We need to say this as a unified voice: parents, educators, employers, civic leaders, white and black and brown and purple leaders, and politicians.

Since that's not going to happen, *you* probably need to stop watching Lou. You need to focus on the fact that the only reason to have an employee is profit and the only kind of employee to have is a profitable one. Further, you want to use the overwhelming majority of your money available for wages to attract exceptional talent for your most important jobs and to reward truly exceptional performance. To do that, you have to be a Scrooge about paying the people who do commoditized, mundane jobs and the people providing only ordinary, barely profitable performance. You have to pay as little as you legally and possibly can for the lowest-level work, in order to, by market comparisons, grossly over pay, over incentivize, and over reward the highly profitable employees doing highly profitable work.

Incidentally, I have nothing personal against Lou Dobbs. I watch him. I sometimes agree with him. I use him here as a symbol of all liberal and populist demagoguery on this issue of wages and wage differentials. In my opinion, an honest discussion of these issues is not occurring anywhere, including in Lou's forum.

We Can Get Even Clearer by Dehumanizing the Equations

Fundamentally, an employee is a rented asset. It has a monthly payment to be made on it. Just like a piece of equipment. So if you are renting a hay baling machine for $300.00 a month but it breaks down all the time, makes the bales the wrong sizes, is slow, and when it's all said and done bales only about $400.00 worth of hay, what should you do with it? Turn it back in. If it costs you $300.00, it had better bale $3,000.00 worth of hay. Because you are in the hay baling business for one reason and one reason only: to make as much money as possible. And you need to remember that the hay business can be good some sunny years but bad some wet years or if there are too many sunny years, and it may even be ruined altogether before long if Al Gore's right about global warming. So in the good years you have to make enough profit for those years plus more, to cover the years you make poor profits or no profits or have to reach into your pockets and put money back into the business. Your hay baler had better give you a big, big return on your investment in it. If it doesn't, you may need a different hay baler. Or you may need to get out of the hay baling business altogether, turn back in all 100 of your hay balers, and find something entirely different to do. That's why it's good to only rent the hay balers, not buy them.

So every piece of equipment—that is, every employee—must pay off at a big multiple of his cost.

Which gets us to employees' cost. Few business owners properly calculate employee cost, because they leave out several very important numbers. Every C.P.A., M.B.A. and others of their ilk I've ever seen gets this wrong. Every management book I've ever read gets it wrong.

Here's how they do it: wages + taxes + benefits + overhead. So, if an employee is paid, let's say $12.00 an hour, and taxes and Social Security and workers' comp and so on add, say, 30%, that puts us at $15.60 an hour. Then add the health care plan, the 401(k) matching contributions, the Christmas bonus, and so on—let's say that calculates out to another $1.00 an hour. Then some neglect overhead, but it belongs in there. Employees use up soap, toilet paper, steal office supplies, require heat and air-conditioning, and take up space. If it costs this hypothetical business owner $2,000.00 a month for his space, utilities, and supplies, and he has four employees, that's $500.00 each divided by 160 work hours, or $3.12 an hour. Now we're up to $19.72 an hour. But we are just getting started.

The REAL Costs

The first big number omitted is the do-over number—the cost of mistakes. Consider the dying American automakers. Among their many problems is a unionized, highly paid, grossly overpaid work force incapable of or unwilling to actually do their jobs right. Consequently these companies are awash in recalls. Hundreds of thousands of cars have to be done over. None of that cost gets taken back out of the incompetent employees' paychecks. The company just eats it. Translation: your employees make mistakes with zero consequences or cost; you bear 100% of the burden for their screwups. And screw up they will. When I took over a terribly troubled manufacturing company, its assembly line mimicked

God's for snowflakes: every item coming off it was different. Employees can, obviously, make and ship defective goods, ship goods to the wrong place, pack goods poorly so they break, damage raw materials, waste materials, annoy and drive away customers, not answer the phone until the eighth ring instead of the third as instructed, thus letting prospects you paid money for give up and hang up, and on and on and on ad infinitum. More importantly, employees not only can but *will* do these things. There is a hard cost in all this that must be factored into the employee cost in advance, because you can't go charge them for their mistakes as they happen.

Obviously, this cost varies by business, by employee, and by employer. No formula for calculating it exists that I know of. But for the sake of this hypothetical example, let's conservatively say that our pretty good employee costs us about $400.00 a week from waste, mistakes, and outright theft. Divide by 40 hours; add $10.00 an hour to the employee's cost. Now we're up to $29.72 an hour.

Next big number all the bean counters ignore and are ignorant of: the cost of YOUR time. With employees comes time *consumption*. In big companies, much of this is easy to see and can be cost controlled, because they employ professional baby-sitters at modest wages (called Human Resources or HRD professionals) and have layers of middle management baby-sitting each other. In a small business, however, the layers are compressed or not there at all, and you are definitely not going to pay $50,000.00 a year or so to an HRD person. So your employees are going to consume your time. As I lay out in this book, they require you to take on three jobs: Leadership, Management, and Supervision. You have to hire, fire, train, coach, police. Break up knife fights (I did that with two computer programmers), listen to marital breakup stories, and this list is long. Again I know of no formula. But let's just say it's an average of two hours a week per employee.

Now, what's your time worth when doing the highest-value things you do? Mine is currently worth $1,600.00 an hour and up. So if an employee sucks up two hours of my time each week, that's $3,200.00 divided into her 40 hours, which adds $80.00 an hour to the cost of having her. Your time is, frankly, probably less valuable than mine. To be simplistic, let's assume you're happy making $100,000.00 a year divided by roughly 2,000 work hours, which makes your time worth $50.00 an hour. If she sucks up two hours of your time this week, that's $100.00 divided into her 40 hours, adding $2.50, which brings her total cost to $32.22 an hour. If, however, you want to make $1,000,000.00 a year . . . .

The final big number is the cost of her absence and replacement. I'm always amused when I'm in Washington, DC, in winter, when they announce that only the *essential* employees should brave the roads and report to work. Shouldn't only essential employees be coming in *every* day? Why is anybody employing a nonessential employee? This tells you a lot about the stupidity that blankets Washington, DC, but it's also telling about the reality of business. Any small-business owner can tell you that if the business can operate for three weeks while Mary or Billy Bob takes family leave days, they aren't needed at all. But if they are needed, you have to replace them when they are absent. You do this by having other employees short and cheat their responsibilities to cover or taking your higher-value time to cover or bringing in temps that cost double or triple Mary's wages. Will she be absent this year? Of course, at least 20 days, combining vacation, personal, and sick time. Then every few years, she'll quit or be fired and you'll incur advertising, hiring, and training costs to replace her. Factor all that in. Let's guess: 20 days of your time used multiplied by your $50.00-an-hour value; $400.00 a day; $8,000.00 a year. Working backward, that comes to approximately $4.00 an hour added to her $32.22, bringing her cost to $36.22.

Well, you had no idea you were actually paying Mary $36.22 an hour, did you?

And that's my point.

I'll bet you'd require more of Mary and manage Mary differently if you did know. Now you do.

ROI

Now to ROI, return on investment. At $36.22 an hour, Mary costs you about $5,795.00 a month or $69,000.00 a year. What sort of return on that investment will be satisfactory to you? If you compare it to bank interest on CDs, then the hurdle is low. Mary need only cover her cost plus a measly $2,700.00 of profit. Of course, if you sold the business and put all the money in bank CDs, you'd never have to even see Mary or any of your other employees again. Chances are, you would like something superior to bank interest just for putting up with your people and occasionally stopping by your own office. But what ROI do you want? Two-to-one, three-to-one, four-to-one. At four-to-one, Mary has to produce $276,000.00 of profit. Is she?

This, finally, gets us to the second most critical managerial decision: How will you quantify and measure the profit produced by Mary? Most business owners will tell me they need Mary and are able to tell me what Mary does, but hardly any can ever tell me how much Mary makes for them.

CHAPTER 7

They ALL Go Lame

"Horse Sense" is the faculty that prevents horses from betting on people.

—UNKNOWN

I own racehorses. At any one time, 15 to 20 of them. I have day-to-day, hands-on personal contact with them. It is impossible not to form relationships with them, to bond more with some than others, to care about them, and to miss them when they leave the stable. Each horse has his own unique personality. Some are antisocial, but most are not only social but real characters. They are equine athletes, each trying his best to perform successfully. Most give it their all—for you. I also drive professionally in more than 100 harness races a year, and I always keep several of these racehorses to drive myself. With these, the bond can be even greater, as I and the horse are competing out there as a team. When I have retired horses, I have gone somewhere private and wept. There are several I miss often, even though they've been gone for years.

With all that said, they can never become pets. This is a business. They are professional equine athletes and I own the team. I must trade players, I must force players to retire, if I am to keep my team competitive and my business solvent. Beyond that, the ultimate truth of owning, training, and racing horses is: they ALL go lame.

As the saying goes, it's not a question of if. It's a question of when.

With the horses, they mostly go lame physically. But some go lame psychologically. They lose their personal passion for competing; they lose their will to win. Or they become overly picky about the conditions required for their peak performance; they refuse to race well in rain or cold or peak summer heat or from outside starting gate positions. One way or another, at some point, they all go lame. If their lameness cannot be quickly and affordably resolved, then they must go. Some go on to other, second careers, as pleasure riding horses, Amish buggy horses, even police horses—as in a long-ago Disney® movie. Others retire to the pasture. Wealthy people with big estates like having retired racehorses as living, breathing, walking lawn ornaments. An unfortunate few with severe and untreatable injuries or unresolvable vicious behavior must be put to sleep. Getting overly attached to any of them is a very bad idea because the day will inevitably come when you must make the decision to send them packing. Key words: *inevitably, must.*

So it is with your employees, associates, partners, and vendors. At some point, every single one of them will go lame. The instances when an entrepreneur goes the distance of his business life with the same person at his side or working for him productively or serving him as a supplier from beginning to end are so rare and extraordinary, they are the stuff of business legends. Walt and Roy Disney and Rich DeVos and Jay Van Andel, co-founders of Amway®, come to mind in the partner category. Hardly any others do. The relative rarity of these long and happy business relationships should convince you not to wager a sou on having one of your own. Know that every single person in your business life will go lame inevitably and you will need to send them packing.

NO B.S. Ruthless Management Truth #3

When a food is no longer edible, it must be thrown out. When an employee is no longer profitable, he must go.

There are even famously productive CEOs, executives, and legendary entrepreneurs who went lame and had to be sent packing by their partners, shareholders, and boards of directors. Famous business leaders celebrated in *Fortune, Forbes, Inc., The Wall Street Journal,* and so on go lame and must be sent packing.

I was a huge fan of Michael Eisner during 80% of his tenure at the Disney helm. He reinvigorated a moribund company. I did very well as a stockholder, thanks to his confident and aggressive leadership. I tell Eisner stories to my clients and coaching group members. Roy Disney made a terrific choice in bringing him in. Roy also made a terrific choice in forcing him out. For whatever combination of reasons, Eisner went lame. He could no longer lead the company effectively, he was alienating critically important allies left and right, he was no longer a profitable employee, and he had to go. When a horse can no longer win, he has to go. When an employee is no longer profitable, he must go.

Lee Iacocca gave Ford the Mustang, one of its most successful products ever and a product as iconic as the Model T. And he was fired. He subsequently saved Chrysler with decisive action, cunning salesmanship, and dynamic leadership. That, however, does not mean that the folks at Ford were necessarily wrong in firing him. Sometimes a person who goes lame and is ineffectual in one environment can be re-born, re-energized, and highly effective in a new environment.

Why and How I Fired Myself

There's a famous Clint Eastwood movie line: A man's got to know his limitations. I think I'm fairly honest about my own limitations. Primarily with my strengths in advertising, marketing, and sales, I built a small but very successful and exceptionally profitable information-marketing business, incorporating my flagship paid subscription newsletter, *The No B.S. Marketing Letter*, other publications, and seminars. It hit a wall, though, largely because of my managerial deficiencies and, even more so, my personal distaste for managing people, especially layers of people and vendors, and my unwillingness to do certain things necessary to take the business to its next logical, evolutionary level. I faced choices of impossible-to-sustain stagnation, riding the business slowly into the ground while siphoning out all the money I could before its last gasp, or firing myself and figuring out how to replace myself in a way much more profitable for the business and, hopefully, financially and personally satisfactory for myself.

I had basically gone lame. I was bored, irritable, and tired with the many business functions and responsibilities that did not play to my strengths, but completely unwilling to hire and manage key people to take over those responsibilities. Personally, I'd rather have a root canal without anesthesia than have employees, and if you think that's odd coming from the author of a book on no-b.s. management, please go back and read the book's introduction; I explain myself there. Anyway, I knew I'd gone lame and that I needed to be sent packing. Since there was nobody to fire me, I fired myself.

I found someone within my clientele who was ably qualified and willing, even eager, to move from running a small, niched business of our kind to a big, expandable mainstream business. He not only possessed marketing knowledge and skills comparable with mine but also had extensive experience hiring, managing, and firing staff, building infrastructure, and overseeing complex operations. He was willing to cross many Rubicons I was not, including ones having to do with staff size, capital investment, internet marketing, and managing thousands of online affiliates. I sold him the business via a formula involving a purchase price, a consulting fee, an ongoing royalty, and opportunities to create new joint ventures, and we reduced and narrowed my responsibilities almost entirely to those things I'm not only exceptionally skilled at but also enjoy and have a passion for doing. As soon as we got the lame guy (me) out of the way, the business began multiplying. I'm delighted to say that, after a first-year pay cut, each successive year has provided me with an escalating income greater than it was when I owned the whole thing myself. Thank you, Bill Glazer.

Such arrangements are not easy to make, such people are not easy to find, and there are caveats about them too numerous and complicated to include here. The main point, however, is that I faced reality about having a lame employee on my hands, in this case the CEO, in this case me. And I not only faced the reality but did something about it.

That's the lesson, or cautionary tale. They all go lame. Even you. When one does go lame, he must be sent packing. Even you.

No farmer long keeps a cow that can't give milk. There's a term for such a cow.

Burgers.

—TOLD TO ME BY A NEIGHBOR WHO OWNED SEVERAL FARMS WHEN I WAS BUT A WEE TYKE

CHAPTER 8

The Worst Number in Business Is . . .

Only the paranoid survive.

—Andy Grove, CEO, Intel

The worst number in business is one. One of just about anything is a bad thing.

In my little home office, where I work under deadline pressure as an advertising copywriter, I do not have one Mac. I have three. Why? So when Mac #1 freezes up, crashes, or requires an exorcism, I can move what I'm working on and urgently need to print out before the day's FedEx deadline to Mac #2. And in case Mac #2 has indigestion or PMS or leprosy that day, I have Mac #3. I keep them in different rooms to prevent contagion. My Mac is my employee. If Mac were a living, breathing human employee who, say, printed what I wrote in booklets on a printing press, I'd want at least two of those Macs and two printing presses. NEVER one.

Yes, this doubles your personnel cost. But that's an easier economic puzzle to solve than is suddenly, abruptly being without the one person absolutely required to deliver a job on time to your most important client or to get tax reports filed before you are fined up the wazoo or to staff your trade show booth this weekend, where you intend writing 30% of your business for the year. I've had clients report their number one and number only salesman calling in to quit the day he was supposed to be jetting off to McCormick Place in Chicago for just such a trade show. And, defying my own rule, by having my wife of some 20 years run my entire office, I was suddenly (because of my own incredible myopia) served with divorce papers, a restraining order barring me from entering my own home, *and* a resignation notice. Fortunately, I had a capable replacement readily available, and my wife was cooperative about the transition, but even so it wasn't pretty, and it could have been a disaster. (For soap opera fans: We were divorced. We've remarried. All is well.) These are not freakish incidents like being bitten in the butt by a snake escaped from your local zoo who has found his way up the pipe to your toilet—still, looking before sitting is prudent. You will be bitten by this "one thing" if you insist on leaving yourself vulnerable to it.

You still refuse to double up? The next best things, poor substitutes but better than no preventive medicine at all, are cross training and, when possible, job sharing or job rotation. Cross training means everybody is trained in everybody else's job. Job sharing means two part-time people do one full-time job. This is a quietly growing, trendy practice in corporate America that actually seems to work. Job rotation means two employees swap jobs during each month; Bill gets Job A the first two weeks and Job B the last two weeks, and Betty gets B and then A. If all that seems awkward to you, wait until you see just how awkward the "I had just one and one is gone" scenario can be.

Recently, a friend of mine with a small business found her assistant and office manager stealing untold amounts of time. Because my friend had taken my advice and had two assistants and co-office managers working for her at the same time, she was able to take the one out back and shoot her. Had she not taken my advice, she'd have been held hostage at gunpoint by her own dysfunctional and thieving employee. **You decide at whose head the gun is pointed.**

Just as a bonus point, one's the worst number for anything else too. Too much of your revenue dependent on one key account, one product, one service, one advertising medium, one calendar event, one means of distribution, one anything, anything, anything.

The Happy Delusion That Bad Things Happen Only to the Other Man's Business

I used to speak 25 to 27 times a year for the largest, most prominent public seminar company in America, pulling crowds of 20,000 to 30,000 to each event. The entire business was wiped out almost overnight, thanks to 9/11. Two events were scheduled the week after, one in New York, both including a famous former U.S. President and other celebrities on the program. The chickenshit former President and several other celebrities cancelled. Attendance was all but nonexistent; thus the vital on-site revenues from book, home study course, and merchandise sales were cut from dollars to pennies. Refund demands went through the roof. Business bankrupt. Why? Total dependence on one way of making money.

Of course, something like 9/11 would never happen to *your* business.

In a business I was running long ago, in a turnaround situation, desperate for every earned dollar, I had a client whose business we depended on tell me he was switching to a competitor over a price difference of several pennies a unit. Even though we had carried him when he had cash flow troubles, promoted him to our other customers, and he and I were personal friends. He said, "You understand, biz is biz."

Of course, *your* most important client would never do such a thing.

A client I'd warned and warned and warned about this "one thing" business was wiped out by a change in the laws governing the use of broadcast fax as an advertising medium. He went from a fat 'n' happy millionaire with hundreds of thousands of dollars flowing in every month to a businessman with no business in less than 30 days. The passage of the Do Not Call List laws decimated the mortgage refi industry, including many of its most successful companies that were overly reliant on cold-call telemarketing. The TV infomercials you see constantly today, that fueled one of my clients' growth of a billion-dollar-a-year business, were once illegal—you could not buy 30 consecutive minutes of commercial time.

Of course, *your* medium that you rely on most could never be taken away from you.

A friend of mine selling more than $500,000.00 worth of his product on a home shopping channel, busily buying second homes and yachts with the money, with manufacturing established in China, and a boatload of goods en route, was abruptly told by the home shopping channel they'd no longer be selling his product; they'd knocked it off, to be sold under a brand name they controlled, by one of their most popular "house" personalities. In 24 hours he went from king of the world to owning a steamship full of doohickeys with no place to sell them.

There's a very big company I dare not identify by name, with a very interesting strategy for acquiring smaller companies at deep discounts. It has used the very same strategy at least 11 times that I know of. It finds a small manufacturer of a unique product or products well protected by patents that its huge direct-to-consumer sales force can move huge quantities of, beginning with a huge surge when the product is first introduced. It gets the little company's owners greed glands so stimulated by the prospect of going from making and selling a small, steady output of units and earning a good living to selling a huge, endless tidal wave of units and getting richer than Trump's ex-wives that these owners agree to onerous contracts imposing all sorts of dire penalties for tardy deliveries or product defects, exclusivity to the big company but with no certain, continuing commitments from it, and other draconian provisions. The big company then buries the small company in orders. The small company's owners scurry frantically to ramp up; they buy and lease equipment, lease more space, hire more people, and go deeply in debt to do it. They quickly cease worrying about their small accounts and leave most of them high and dry without product. Then the big company announces it's going to abruptly terminate the relationship and manufacture a substitute product internally . . . or it might, *might* consider buying the small company. The little company's owners can face horrible destruction, epic financial losses, quite possibly working for free for years just to crawl out from under all the debt, or they can sell the company for debt transfer plus a pittance of its previous, true value and get out alive.

> **Of course, *your* distribution would never be taken away from you. Of course, *you'd* never get taken advantage of in such a devious way. *You'd* never be blinded by greed.**

Burglaries and fires happen only to the neighbors down the street. Only other people's teenagers get arrested for drunken driving or possession of drugs. Go ahead, live in denial. Believe your business somehow impervious to the myriad of "one thing" disasters that befall all others. Go ahead.

Just because you're paranoid doesn't mean they're not out to get you.

—Dr. Charlie Jarvis

CHAPTER 9

Hire Slow, Fire Fast

Whoever admits that he is too busy to improve his methods has acknowledged himself to be at the end of his rope. And that is the saddest predicament.

—J. OGDEN ARMOUR

I first heard "Hire slow, fire fast" from Chuck Sekeres, the founder of a very successful company, Physicians Weight Loss Centers. He was attending my seminar, but when it came out of his mouth, I scribbled it down. It's at least as profound as anything Aristotle ever said. Its genius and its truth is that it's polar opposite to what 99% of us do. (Oh, yeah, I've been guilty of this one a few times myself. And it cost me dearly.)

So, as an aside, here's the single most useful and empowering piece of success advice I have ever heard in my entire life. I've based most of what I've done in my own business life and in developing strategies for my clients on this single piece of advice.

I heard this one while still a teenager, listening to a cassette tape by Earl Nightingale. Earl said that if you wanted to do something—anything—successfully, and you had no instructions, no role model, no road map, and no mentors, all you needed to do was look around at how the majority was doing that thing, then do the opposite—because the majority is always wrong. Whenever I teach this, there's always one twit who challenges me with our own great American democracy as his sword. After all, he'll say, our system of government is based on majority rule. Well, no it's not. First of all, the founding fathers originally had only the people paying taxes—at the time, land owners—voting, as it should be today. Second, the electoral college got stuck in to provide a last line of defense against public stupidity—in case you didn't know it, the electors aren't legally bound to vote as their state's majority has. Third, fortunately, the majority does not vote. If the majority actually, directly elected people, Britney Spears would be President and Paris Hilton would be Vice President. So, no, thank our stars, our government is not majority rule. And the principle stands that the majority is always wrong, and you gain most by conforming to the majority as little as possible. (For more from me on this, take a gander at www.RenegadeMillionaire.com.)

NO B.S. Ruthless Management Truth #4

The majority is always wrong.

Now back to this hiring and firing thing.

Most business owners fire slow. They manage like they go to the movies. Sitting through a three-hour-long movie that is rancid from 1st to 180th minute. Why? They think it has to get better. They keep hoping it will get better. Because I'm a Burt Reynolds fan, I once did this with the single worst movie ever made, *At Long Last Love* or something like that, in which Burt and Cybill Shepherd sing and dance. Bad employees do not cure themselves like ham hung in a barn. Hope isn't a sound business strategy. But that's what too many managers do. Wait and hope for a miraculous, spontaneous cure. Consequently, according to my admittedly unscientific survey of about a hundred of my clients, the average firing occurs somewhere between 6 and 18 months *after* the business owner *knew* the employee was consistently performing poorly, consistently noncompliant, poisoning the workplace and negatively affecting others in it, or otherwise stinking up the joint. Ironically, most employees who finally get fired are mystified the axe didn't fall sooner. One told a friend of mine, "When you didn't fire me five months ago when you should have, I figured I could get away with just about anything." Some fired employees are even relieved and glad it's over; they've been visualizing the sword of Damocles overhead for months.

Being 6 to 18 months late doing anything in business is a very bad idea.

There is, sadly, one other reason the necessary firings occur so late. Sure, we're waiting and hoping for the bad movie to get good, against our best instincts and all our previous experience. But beyond that, a lot of owners delay firing people who desperately need firing because the business owner is lazy. He has permitted the bad employee to amass and control information only he knows, carried in his head or filed with his own unique code. One lawyer told me, "She's my worst employee but I rely on her every time I go to court." Huh? And the business owner dreads the difficulty of finding and training a replacement. In this, he's like the single guy at home alone on an autumn Sunday afternoon in dirty underwear, watching football, who discovers he has no cash and his refrigerator has only a beer, a two-day-old half of a pizza, and some bologna going green around the edges. After weighing the options, he'd rather trim the green and eat the bologna and old pizza for dinner than find clothes, get dressed, go to the ATM, then go to the grocery store. Hard to have any sympathy for him when he's up half the night at the vomitorium.

Being 6 to 18 months late is inexcusable.

Next mistake: hiring fast. This is closely linked to the first mistake more often than not. Finally firing the toxic employee, you create a vacancy. It needs to be filled. You've done nothing proactive to be able to fill it until your urgent and desperate need has arisen. Thus the fact that your "best" applicant attracted from your first help-wanted posting at Monster.com has two nose rings, sports a tattoo that says "Kill the Boss," has no references, and occasionally interrupts her sentences by snarling like a dog is ignored. Hey, those phones need answering *today*.

This is the way almost everybody operates. Do the opposite.

CHAPTER 10

Critical Factor #412: How to Find Useful Employees and Vendors

By Scott Tucker

There are at least 500 Critical Factors that I know of for managing a business for maximum profit. One of the most critical is the finding of useful employees and vendors. You can't live with 'em but you can't live without 'em. Or that's how it seems. Pretty early on in any successful venture as an entrepreneur, you come up against a wall you often didn't know was there—or, more likely, you knew it was there but were doing your best to ignore it.

Fact is, no matter how good you are, how hard and fast you work, there's a limit on what you can do all by yourself. Even when you've got everything automated to the nth degree, you're still up against limitations of time and space. There are only so many hours in a day, you've got two hands max, and you can't be in two places at once. I know. I've tried.

I run my entire operation with just one employee. I have five corporations, all under one roof. Just one employee. I can do this because I am careful and deliberate about how I hire, deal with, and ultimately fire employee(s) and vendors.

I've learned a thing or two along the way and stumbled into a few blind alleys and dead ends in the process. My hope is in the next few pages that what I've learned from it all will be of some benefit you.

Bottom line: you can make a high income, but you can't get *really* rich doing it all yourself. I know that what you *want* to do is to control every little detail. Your "inner control freak" just doesn't want to let go.

So what's the answer? You can do one of two things . . .

You can either limit your income and success or buckle up, knuckle down, and get hiring or outsourcing!

Hiring is a minefield. And a really easy one to step in! The hiring part is easy. Actually way too easy. Most business owners hire too quickly, too casually—and, by hiring, I mean actually hiring employees or selecting vendors or freelancers. "Easy hiring" makes the managing all the more difficult. Then, all too often, the biggest problem is firing. That usually gets tackled only long after it should have been solved, and long after all the other problems that led to this problem in the first place have wreaked havoc in your business!

No doubt about it: having employees *can* suck up massive amounts of time and resources, far out of proportion to the benefits they bring. Get the wrong person in the job, and you've really done it to yourself.

The first thing you need to realize about employees is that they are the *hired* help. They're there for a check. That's their prime motivation. That's fundamentally it. That is the basis for the entire relationship.

One of the first things I teach the business owners who are in my coaching groups is: get an assistant, but get the right one! It's *always* a bad idea to hire someone for a job just because he's your best buddy or your sister's husband. The closer we are to someone, the harder it can be to enforce strict boundaries without it becoming personal. In fact, you shouldn't hire *anyone* for *any* job unless he has the personality and mindset for it, and preferably the skills, too; although when you find a winner, he'll be eager to learn *any* skills he needs but doesn't yet have. And you'd be a fool to pass him up.

The second thing you need to realize is if you go down the normal route of finding, hiring, managing, and ultimately firing employees, then you're going to suffer the same consequences as everyone else.

To have a *different* "employee experience," you've got to approach the whole thing in a *different* way. Cuz the majority is always wrong.

No Excuses

You need to treat your business like a military operation, applying military standards of responsibility and accountability to employees and vendors, demanding results and accepting no excuses. And if you've never read Elbert Hubbard's "A Message to Garcia," now would be a good time to do it.

Excuses don't pay the bills, excuses don't get your orders taken and fulfilled. Excuses don't and never will keep your customers and clients happy. And if you don't keep your customers and clients happy, you won't have a business for very long at all.

I'm staggered at the amount of business owners who shy away from this process of elimination and it's one thing I'm really tough on with my clients.

You have to take a firm line with your employees and stick to it. There is no room for mercy here. No one is going to feel the same way about your business as you do, and no one has got the same bet riding on it—if it goes belly-up, your employees can just go find another job, but you're on the hook here. Sure, you can show a little give-and-take *if* and *only if* they're worth it. Someone who's habitually late, incompetent, and dishonest and requires constant supervision doesn't qualify for mercy. You need to cut him loose quickly, just like you'd cut out a cancer.

Your "No Excuses" policy must be stated and made clear at the very beginning of any relationship. In the job interview or first meeting with a potential supplier. In written employee policies or in a "relationship confirming letter" to a new vendor. There can't be any confusion over the fact that you don't cut anybody any slack.

How to Hunt

Whatever you invest in getting only high-quality people will pay you back hundreds of times over! You'll find few things as expensive, time-consuming, and painful as winding up with the employee from hell. The same is true of vendors and of clients, too, of course. You'll find few things as profitable as winding up with employees and suppliers who thoroughly understand you and your expectations and work to meet them.

OK, so how do you separate the diamonds from the gravel? Your goal is to get the maximum results from the minimum amount of time and effort on your part.

Fortunately, finding competent and effective employees or vendors boils down to a *marketing* exercise, just the same as finding customers and clients does.

Just like an online dating ad, this is no time to be squeamish about saying exactly what you want. And possibly more important than that, exactly what you *don't* want. This goes against conventional wisdom but is completely in line with "Take-Away Selling"*—the *harder* you make it for prospective employees or vendors to apply, the *better*-quality applicants you're going to get.

People who'd just "like the job," and who would be inclined to fill out a simple online application form or drop into your place of business and fill out an application or mail in a predone resume, are not ardent and earnest enough for your purposes and can be easily repelled by putting a few unique hurdles in their way.

---

*Refers to Chapter 21, page 327, in *No B.S. Sales Success Book*, by Dan Kennedy.

On the other hand, you know anyone who's managed to navigate his way through a series of tasks is able to follow directions, willing to follow directions, and highly motivated to secure a good opportunity.

So make them follow "clear, yet confusing" instructions. One technique I suggest my coaching Members use is to say in a classified ad to call a 24-hour toll-free recorded message. The message tells them what to do, in exacting detail. But it also sets them up to mess up, and to fail the "test" that this process actually is.

Most won't even realize that all this is a test.

For instance, the recorded message might say, "Do not fax your resume to (xxx) xxx-xxxx [competitor's fax machine]. Do not e-mail your resume to x@x.com [competitor's e-mail address]. Do not call by phone at (xxx) xxx-xxxx [competitor's phone number]. Instead, please send your two-page letter not by postal mail, DHL, or UPS, but by FedEx only, to 123 Main Street, Anytown, Anystate, zip code [your nonpostal mailbox service]."

My instructions above were 100% clear, but try finding someone to follow them! What's great about this is it tests everyone for you. You won't get a great "response rate" because all the knuckleheads will bug everyone but you! And that's just the way we want it!

Most won't want to go through the trouble to send a FedEx, and that's great! Those you do hear from will have shown a number of key ingredients you're looking for in an employee.

You'll weed out an awful lot of people this way—people who can't or won't follow your instructions, whom you wouldn't want working in your business anyhow! And the ones who *do* get through this process are more likely to do as you tell them (and isn't that kind of the whole idea?).

Make your ad and your response mechanism do the "hard work" for you! Remember, finding staff is a marketing exercise, so treat it like one.

The more you can do to separate the wheat from the chaff, automatically and early on, the better results you're going to get. Some of my coaching Members who use this System send prospective employees to the library, via their free recorded messages. They give the prospective employees a "homework assignment"! It's all right on the recording. They never even talk to the tire kickers themselves! They just get the FedExes.

And that's exactly what you want, because by the time you have to sit down and start making decisions, you'll be choosing only from highly-motivated, highly-qualified candidates.

And again, you can use a similar mechanism to obtain suppliers. Instead of a classified or display ad, you might send out a letter. It invites the vendor to apply to provide services to you and gives similar instructions for the one and only way you will accept their application.

OK, so you've thinned the herd and ruthlessly cut out the deadwood. The guy or gal in front of you (on paper) *seems* "perfect." You're done, right?

Wrong.

All you've done so far is dug out some desirable traits—now you've got to do some real homework (or hire it out)! What you need to do now is some background checking. You might feel uncomfortable about this, or think it unnecessary, but believe me, it's a lot less painful than getting it wrong. Cheaper, too!

First, one common trait all the best employees have is they come from a background where there was a business in their family. Maybe Mom and Pop owned a business, or an uncle or even an older sibling.

They've had to work. They know what work is.

Or, try this: is your applicant the eldest child of an alcoholic parent? I find that the eldest child of an alcoholic grew up having to keep the house together. He had to grow up quick, take on responsibility, and so on.

I think it is a similar situation if the applicant was an only child, because he had to grow up self-reliant, independent . . . think "latchkey kid." The advantage here is he won't need a lot of hand-holding from you. He won't sit around waiting for someone else to take care of something.

Drug users? Nonrecovering alcoholics? You don't want them working for you. If they need help, fine, but they need to get that help before you take them on. And, remember, you can't help someone who doesn't (yet) want help.

Beyond the issues of unreliability, there could be a motivation for embezzlement, product theft, and so on.

Make a drug test a mandatory requirement of your application process. No, you're not infringing on their rights; they don't have to take the test, and you don't have to hire folks unwilling to be tested.

Are the applicants honorably discharged military veterans? They'll have an original form DD-214 to prove it if they served in the U.S. military. And make sure on the honorable part too. Make them produce the form. Don't just take their word for it.

If they have experience in the military, you should take this as a plus. Attention to detail, deadlines, and a "no excuses, get it done" attitude are all taught and enforced there. They come trained. And you don't have to train them on those values yourself. Plus, they're punctual. They actual show up *early*, not just on time! And they've worked in difficult environments, for a meager salary. They aren't clock watchers.

They've been trained, at tax payers' expense, to follow instructions and procedures. And they'll have initiative and personal responsibility, along with a healthy dose of unselfish teamwork, drummed into them.

So now you've pruned and ruthlessly cut the boneheads, deadbeats, no-hopers, and morons out of the loop, grilled one or two people at length, done some digging, and decided on the "right" one.

Hold on here . . . because you're *still* not done.

You don't design an airplane and fill it full of passengers without taking it for some test flights first, do you?

That's why you need to have some kind of "probationary" period where the applicants prove their worth. Again, you can't be squeamish about this. Don't be afraid to fire and go all the way back to square one. It always pays you back in the long run.

For me the quickest and easiest acid test in any business relationship is *punctuality*. If an employee or vendor, or even a client, can't be on time for telephone appointments or interviews, what *else* is he going to screw up?

Don't work with people who can't be on time. If you *do* then you *will* suffer unpleasant consequences, and probably sooner rather than later. If an applicant is late, drop 'em. That's it. No second chance. Bye-bye.

The second thing is to give them something pretty easy to do, a simple performance test before you agree to work with them and put anything of monumental importance in their hands. People's habits are ingrained, and someone with attention to detail and good problem-solving skills will apply them equally to small tasks and big ones.

Don't allow yourself to be sucked in and fooled by excuses. If they screw up now, they'll screw up later.

Like it or not, the point will come where your workload is going to outgrow your ability to cope with it alone. And finding good employees and vendors is easy, so long as you take my advice. I know from experience that good employees and vendors are worth their weight in gold, if not more!

Final thought: Whether you're dealing with employees or vendors, the most important thing is to keep control. And to keep control, you've got to keep paying attention. Even the best employees and vendors will screw up, and few will own up to it willingly.

Ultimately it's *your* business and *your* livelihood.

Don't be afraid to fire *anyone* if the situation arises. As the saying goes: *hire slow, fire fast*.

SCOTT TUCKER has achieved exceptional success as a subprime mortgage broker. He now provides seminars, coaching, consulting, and marketing services for mortgage brokers and loan officers throughout the United States and Canada. Visit www.MortgageMarketingGenius.com for information. Only after reviewing that web site, Scott may be reached, via fax only, at (773) 327-2842.

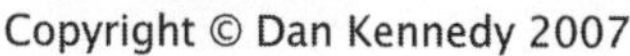

Vincent Palko
www.AdToons.com

CHAPTER 11

Leadership Is Vastly Over-Rated

A leader is one who makes an immediate decision and is sometimes right.

—Elbert Hubbard

Leadership is a powerful buzzword, doubly so since the 9/11 attacks. In politics, we use it as a noun and as an attribute, as in "Rudy Giuliani exhibits real leadership." Supposedly the American public is longing for leadership. If challenged to define it, I doubt many could tell us exactly what it is that they want delivered under its banner. After all, at least half the country was thoroughly pissed off at President Bush as I wrote this, yet, by most attempts at defining *leadership*, he has exhibited plenty of it. He's got a visionary idea of re-making the entire Middle East as the best means of safeguarding America and the world from ever-rising terrorism, he's stuck to his convictions in spite of mounting criticism and opposition (many would say reality), he's defied preferences of members of his own party as well as the opposing party to do what he believes is right, he has, at least on occasions, taken bold action. So why isn't everybody who loves the idea of leadership in love with President Bush?

Because the *idea* of leadership is attractive, but the choices made by somebody acting out leadership are likely to be controversial, even extreme, and there's no way to objectively evaluate them. One man's leadership admired by some is just as easily criticized by others as pigheaded. One man's visionary leadership some find awe inspiring, others find fantastical. In historical retrospect, President Kennedy is revered as a visionary and courageous leader for setting the goal of landing men on the moon and doing it. You heard and hear little if any criticism for misdirecting billions of dollars that might have been better deployed on the war on poverty or securing Social Security or researching cures for Alzheimer's or cancer, although I could certainly make that case. Why the absence of such criticism? JFK was a popular, charismatic individual who chose a mission built around a very simple idea that was subsequently achieved without significant problems, and no astronauts returned to earth as corpses in body bags. It made for terrific TV, too. The public likes good TV. Hates bad TV. President Bush's equally ambitious but land-based pet project has not been so well received for many reasons, and I'm not here to defend it. I only want to point out that, if you can be objective about it for a moment, there are far more similarities than differences in the two Presidents' grandiose schemes, and both could be shown as parallel examples of this longed-for leadership.

In corporate America, leadership—better yet, visionary leadership—is the all-time favorite idea people never tire of talking about. If you laid all the books written about it end to end, I imagine you could walk to the moon. CEOs are frequently glorified as great leaders, then later chastised as arrogant fools by the same media, and finally fired by their boards of directors. Still, everybody loves the endless pursuit of leadership. And that's the rub. The pursuit is endless because there's no definable, definite target. Leadership is so ethereal nobody can agree on what it is, nobody's sure if he's got it or not, and nobody can quantify its value. I've certainly worked with highly profitable businesses run by people I'd rank as pathetically inferior leaders. I've also known people who seem to exhibit all the characteristics ascribed to great leaders but run businesses right into bankruptcy court. Repeatedly.

After much thought, I have come to the conclusion that leadership is vastly overrated. In business, to maximize profits, things that can be agreed on, accurately measured, and proven to deliver predictable results consistently—regardless of who has got his hand on the wheel—are far more valuable. One of these far more valuable assets is systems and procedures, coupled with enforcement (see: Chapters 13 and 14).

McDonald's® is able to deliver millions of products to millions of customers day in, day out, in outlets scattered all over the country, owned by independent operators, without poisoning a lot of people, with consistent (albeit mediocre, but satisfactory) quality, at value prices, and dominate its field—all with pimply faced, hormones-raging, MTV-attention-deficitent teenagers NOT because of visionary leadership, charismatic leaders, and motivational speakers, or happy-talk team-building campouts. This improbable achievement occurs because of systems.

As an investor, I'd rather invest in a corporation with great systems than one with great leaders. The leaders might all die in a plane crash and leave me with my stock certificates in one hand, hankie in the other. The systems live on. Disney®, a company I own stock in and admire, has had benefit of CEOs generally viewed, at least for a time, as great visionary leaders, although I doubt you'd call Bob Iger "charismatic." However, I've really studied Disney® intently and indepth, and by far, the company's greatest asset is its incredibly sophisticated, microdetailed, micromanaged systems for maximizing profits in every nook and cranny of its parks, with every intellectual property, from every job and every person.

You can probably win a lot of games with any offensive scheme if you have Peyton Manning or Tom Brady as your quarterback. But the reason the West Coast Offense originally designed by Bill Walsh is so much copied is it permits winning games not just with a Joe Montana but with a Steve Young, and even a Steve Bono. Arguably it makes average quarterbacks better. Walsh made the game and the position less about individual personality or exceptional talent and more about the system. Of course it helps to have a Montana or a Young. But . . .

> **. . . the fact of business life is you <u>can't</u> go far if you require *exceptional* people.**

There aren't enough of them to go around. There's intense competition for them. They're expensive. They're damnably hard to keep. If you need only 1 or 2, maybe. But if you need 10 or 20 or more, then you have to get the idea of finding and hiring only superstars and building a team of superstars out of your head.

Exceptional people respond exceptionally well to great leadership. Match some truly exceptional players with an exceptional leader and look out—think the Michael Jordan championship-era Chicago Bulls and Phil Jackson, or the Jimmy Johnson-coached Dallas Cowboys. But if you read Phil Jackson's book and try applying his Zenlike leadership philosophy to a bunch of ordinary employees, you're in for rough sailing. You may need more than Zen meditation to survive it. More like a few stiff drinks. And, by the way, exceptional people can thrive with bad leadership, mediocre leadership, or no leadership at all, too. Think Barry Switzer "leading" the Cowboys to the Super Bowl.

The majority of the people you'll be trying to win in business with are just not going to be exceptional. Not exceptionally motivated or dedicated or ambitious. Not exceptionally skilled or talented. Not exceptionally intelligent. Not exceptionally anything. They will, at best, be average. And average people don't respond well to the "leadership" that excites exceptional people.

There's still a place for the much ballyhooed, much yakked about, much admired "leadership," but to think it is some elusive but magical potion that if gotten just right, like lightning in a bottle, will transform your collection of average folks into eager-beaver, highly responsible superstars is delusional. People putting on grandiose leadership seminars love to sell this fantasy. A lot of executives and business owners like buying it, too, because it's fun to talk about leadership but not a lot of fun to be armpit deep in the minutiae of systems and their enforcement. It's ego satisfying to view oneself as a great leader dedicated to great leadership and then blame the troops for being such unresponsive mallet heads they don't appreciate you; it's not at all ego satisfying to blame yourself for poor systems and weak enforcement. So the next faddish brand of "leadership hocus-pocus" is being thought up as we speak. But if you really want to get your business producing maximum profits with the people you're really going to have to work with in real-world conditions, you'll skip the seminar.

Vincent Palko
www.AdToons.com

CHAPTER 12

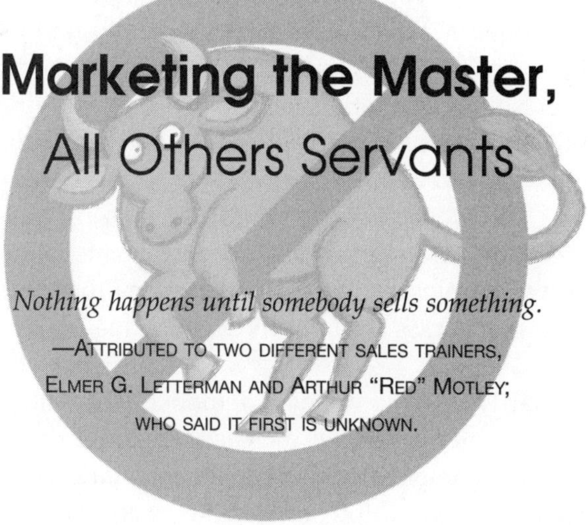

Marketing the Master, All Others Servants

Nothing happens until somebody sells something.

—ATTRIBUTED TO TWO DIFFERENT SALES TRAINERS, ELMER G. LETTERMAN AND ARTHUR "RED" MOTLEY; WHO SAID IT FIRST IS UNKNOWN.

Several years ago, I (foolishly) agreed to personally conduct a "staff training program" for key employees of about a dozen of my clients. They sent them to me as a group for two days. Their employers weren't there. And boy did I get an earful of things I didn't want to hear. It might seem surprising they'd be as candid with me as they were, but their honesty was due, in large part, to the fact they didn't even realize how damaging and incriminating much of what they were stating was. As an example, the majority complained bitterly about two things: (1) having their "real work" and "important work" constantly or unpredictably interrupted by "customers" calling up, e-mailing, or coming in and (2) having their "real work" disrupted by their bosses' decisions to quickly implement an extra promotion or sales effort.

If this surprises you, it shouldn't. I can assure you that your thoughts about what the important work is in your business and your employees' thoughts on this subject are miles apart.

Further, sound marketing, promotion, and sales ideas, initiatives, and projects are constantly sabotaged by operational concerns and employees who view every such thing as "more work."

I have sat in meetings and listened as clients were assaulted by their own employees' barrage of reasons that "we can't do that." Their businesses are literally being managed by the "can't do" plan.

In one fairly large company, I demonstrated with reasonable certainty that sales could be increased by 50% or more if the prospective customers booked by its telemarketing center to come into showrooms at preset times were accurately accounted for, with hour-by-hour reporting from the remote showrooms back to the corporate headquarters, so a series of follow-up steps including e-mail, direct mail, and telemarketing could occur in quick succession with every prospect who failed to show up as promised. The regional sales managers told the company's president such a thing couldn't be done because the salespeople would never accurately account for who was there and who wasn't, thus accounting for how many presentations they made and revealing their true closing percentages. The vice president of sales said it couldn't be done because of the complexity of handling all that feedback and triggering the proper follow-up steps. The vice president of finance said it couldn't be done because half the remote sites weren't equipped with internet-connected laptops and there was no budget for them. A manager of the printing department insisted they could never get the customized mailings out on a timely basis. And some other manager insisted that her "entire data processing department would mutiny if asked to do anything this complicated and time sensitive."

I watched the CEO shrink and surrender. A strong, able-bodied 6-foot, 2-inch man with a matching tie and pocket hankie and a management degree from Stanford reduced to a melted puddle of pinstriped mush. His army of can't-doers left triumphant. I was embarrassed for him.

The kindest description of this is "operations controlling marketing." It should always be the other way around. Why? Because marketing is what brings in the money. As the business owner or president or other-titled leader, your paramount job is to figure out what the best, strongest, most powerful, most effective advertising, marketing, and sales strategies are—and then demand that they be implemented. If they create a lot of operational challenges, difficulty, and even chaos, so be it. Whatever is required has to happen. If the beautiful full-color charts of how things are done have to be thrown out and redrawn, if job descriptions need to be rewritten, if people with inappropriate skills or resistant attitudes must be replaced by fresh troops, if funds must be diverted from other expenditures, so be it. **Best marketing rules; all others are its servants.**

I no longer tolerate this crap from the clients who pay me. If I determine the best mailing we can do for a client's particular promotion needs to go in a 7-inch long tube made of neon green plastic, into which we are going to stuff bags of peanuts along with the sales letter that directs people to a new web site, my

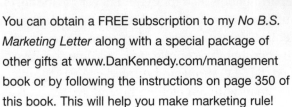

Recommended Resource #2

You can obtain a FREE subscription to my *No B.S. Marketing Letter* along with a special package of other gifts at www.DanKennedy.com/management book or by following the instructions on page 350 of this book. This will help you make marketing rule!

client knows better than to tell me his vendor stocks only 4-inch and 6-inch tubes or ask if cheaper cardboard can be substituted for the plastic or to tell me that there's a peanut shortage in his town due to rampaging elephants or that his web site builder has suddenly been stricken blind. My clients know if they tell me anything of the sort, I'll fire *them*!

Presumably they have found ways to impress a certain reality upon their people that the CEO described earlier was unable to convey to his; the job of management, of folks in operations, heck, of everybody around here, is to invent solutions, not construct roadblocks; is to support marketing, not sabotage it; is to help a new opportunity rise and walk rather than wrestle it to the ground and club it to death.

You have to very firmly decide what imperative is going to govern your business, the employees in it, and the vendors who serve it. There can be only one number-one imperative. Only one master.

For many businesses, sadly, the number one imperative is the can't-do crowd's protection of the status quo and avoidance of difficult challenges, heightened pressure to perform, stress of change, and demand for creative thinking. Their number one imperative is collecting next Friday's paycheck without any disruption of their routines, new learning curves, or "extra" work.

In many other businesses, incredibly, the number one imperative is keeping peace with the staff. I hear about this from many small-business owners—they shake their heads and say, "It just isn't worth the grief it'll cause me in the office." These owners are *whipped*. The governing imperative is the convenience and comfort of *the staff*. A doctor told me that even though he got lots of requests from new patients for initial appointments on Friday afternoons, he couldn't take them because his staff wanted to leave early on Fridays. Tuesday and Wednesday mornings were nearly devoid of patients and I saw staff members sitting around reading magazines. The week needed to be re-arranged for Monday and Thursday 9:00 to 5:00, Tuesday and Wednesday 11:00 to 5:00, and Friday 10:00 to 6:00 P.M.

In other businesses, in bizarre logic, the number one imperative is what's cheapest rather than what delivers the best return on investment. In some businesses, the governing imperative is entrenched logistics. *We can't do this because the vendor we use . . . the software program we use . . . the delivery service we use won't or can't*. Bye-bye. Next.

Again, you have to very firmly decide what imperative is going to govern your business, the employees in it, and the vendors who serve it. There can be only one number one imperative. If you want maximum profits, that imperative had better be maximum profits. It won't take much analysis to determine the number one imperative governing profits. To save you the trouble of looking, it's having the most effective marketing, to attract new customers, to optimize the value of customers, and to rescue lost customers.

Again, there can be only one master. Its name is Marketing. All others bow and say, "Yes, Master. How may I serve thee, Master?"

CHAPTER 13

Mice at Play

REGULATION #22: Loafing, loitering, visiting or unauthorized absence from work will result in disciplinary action, and may result in loss of your job, and withholding of a good time.

—INSTITUTION RULES AND REGULATIONS, ALCATRAZ

My friend Lee Milteer checked the internet browsing history on one of her employee's computers in the office. The most recent 30 stops were at MySpace.com. Given that there had been previous incidents of on-the-job theft, the employee was fired.

Yes, it's theft, and it's rampant and epic. It's time theft, which you need to look at exactly the same way as cash theft—or you haven't got a fighting chance.

Online community businesses like MySpace and e-commerce giants from Amazon.com to eBay would be starving shadows of themselves were it not for all the daytime use by employees at work, effectively stealing from their employers while playing on the internet. In fact, these companies don't really, truly *make* the lion's share of their money at all. They merely are the beneficiaries of a theft and transfer of productivity from other businesses, including yours. If every employer in America suddenly did what they should do and stopped all workplace access to these sites, and these sites were totally dependent on use by their customers on their own time instead of their employers' time, many of these online entertainment and shopping businesses would dry up and disappear.

As an author, I selfishly love Amazon.com, B&N.com, and other online booksellers. As an Amazon.com stockholder, I've done well. But make no mistake: MySpace.com, eHarmony.com, Amazon.com, Buy.com, and so on are your mortal enemies in your battle to get a just, fair, and full day's work for a full day's pay. And make no mistake: while the cat's not watching, the mice are at play at these web sites, playing computer games, doing their personal banking online, sending e-mail greeting cards, text-messaging friends, and watching movies, while your business phones go unanswered, your customers get treated as annoying interruptions, paperwork gets hidden and buried.

Many of my clients are entrepreneurs with small offices, with one to several employees. These cats work mostly from home and often travel, leaving the mice unsupervised for days on end. Were they able to snoop on their offices, they'd be horrified. When, at my urging, they pull surprise visits or send in someone else unannounced and unknown to the office, they are horrified at what they discover. When they do as I urge and run weekend raids, snooping in desk drawers, file cabinets, appointment books, and computers, they are amazed and, again, horrified at what they find. Spending the workday making friends at MySpace.com is mild, in the grand scheme of things. The mice are doing much worse.

Other clients have professional practices, retail stores, or open-to-public offices like insurance agencies or real estate offices. These cats are also often absent, in the back room drilling teeth, or in the car driving to and from appointments. When we have their businesses mystery shopped by phone or in-person visitors, we uncover mice not only at play but actually quite deliberately sabotaging the business. For example, it's a common and frequent "catch" in professional offices any day the cat's out to find the mice putting all the phones on hold for hours at a time while they play on the computer and talk to boyfriends, girlfriends, and spouses on cell phones. Frustrated callers take their business elsewhere.

Oh, and you don't need to take my word for it. ABC's *20/20* did an outstanding show on this, where they hired people to do on-the-street surveys and then secretly watched their work. They let employees in an ice-cream shop believe the owner was going out of town for the entire day, then observed their work with hidden cameras and sent in mystery shoppers. And so on. Out of all the employees we saw on this show, only one actually did the work she was supposed to do without goofing off and cheating to cover it up—and she was urged by the other employees to stop. The survey takers met the ridiculously low, easy quota by filling out many surveys themselves, then one took a nap on a park bench, another went shopping, and several took lunch breaks much longer than allowed. They falsified their work, defeating its purpose, skewing the results. When shown they were caught, *they were unashamed.* They each had an excuse, from shyness to feeling demeaned by having to do the work. But they all took the money. The ice-cream store employees sat talking to each other while the phone rang endlessly. None of this was rigged. It was and is reality.

Of course, everybody says, "Not MY employees."

Sorry. Mice are mice.

So.

What I suggest is to first of all create a "productivity-only workplace," with distractions removed. Second, the cat must never be away. I'll explain what I mean.

It's Called a Workplace for a Reason

Idea #1: Employees have lockers.

On arrival at Work, Betty and Bobby are required to put all their personal stuff in their lockers. That includes, in most cases, cell phones or any other personal communication devices (including Star Trek™ walkie-talkies), video game doohickeys, lipstick, toenail clippers, snacks, and every other damned thing not used for Work in their Workplace. This means, for example, that the sales clerk at the jewelry counter in Kohl's® won't be yakking away on her cell phone while a customer is standing there waiting. This means your employee won't be text-messaging or gaming or eating when he is supposed to be—what? Say it with me in unison: W-O-R-K-I-N-G.

On breaks, they can go to their lockers, get their personal stuff, and do all the personal things they want, in the break area, employee lounge, parking lot (for the smokers), or wherever else you have for them to go when not working. You might want to set up a really nice space for their personal times, too. A couple of 52-inch flat-screen TVs. Some computers they can use to do their banking, buy shoes, play games. You might even want to give slightly longer breaks. That'd be a great trade-off to keep personal stuff in personal time and place and out of work time and place. If you do all that nice stuff, that's nice. But it's really not necessary. After all, you didn't bring them in to play, did you? You brought them into your business for the day to do what? Say it with me in unison: W-O-R-K.

Oh, and by the way, the speed and pace and demand of W-O-R-K are supposed to make you tired. At the end of a workday, you should actually feel like you worked. As I mentioned previously, I own harness racing horses, and I drive professionally too. Nothing's more irritating to me than sitting in that sulky going back to the barn after a race we didn't win behind a horse that isn't really, really tired.

Of course, there have to be modifications made for different folks in different jobs. But you ought to very carefully consider them and reluctantly make them. Every exception weakens your rule. Through every loophole leaks productivity and, thus, profit.

Idea #2: Everybody doesn't need to be hooked up to the internet.

If Betty and Bobby use their desktop computers to enter data or do accounting work, they need computers. They don't need e-mail and access to MySpace.com. In a decent-sized office with a number of employees, were it me, there'd be one computer hooked up to send and receive e-mail, in a Communications Room, that you went and logged on to and used only when you actually needed to send a message. Think of it like a fax machine. If Betty does a lot of research online, OK, maybe Betty needs hers hooked up. But just because Betty does, Bobby doesn't. And no, your people do not need to be e-mailing and text-messaging each other every other minute all day long either. They can learn to "clump" the items they need to discuss with each other, and actually talk, like, once a day. Although, of course, you can have an intranet without having everybody hooked to the internet.

Idea #3: The cat never leaves.

I am not at all in favor of Big Brother watching me in my private affairs and personal life, so I certainly understand other people objecting to such invasion of their privacy. Heck, I still refuse to use grocery store discount thingamajigs because it irks me they have a record of what sinus remedy or magazine I buy. Politically, I'm as close to a Libertarian as you can be without simply abandoning any practical participation in politics. But note the words: *personal life.* Personal life occurs during personal time in personal space. In public places, people need to grasp that they have no right to privacy, and we should have surveillance cameras in public places like busy streets, so we can prevent terrorist incidents and quickly apprehend terrorists, just like they do in London—and did, for example, in July 2007. In the workplace, people need to grasp that they are there to work, and they have no right to expect privacy; *whatever* they're doing is *your* business as long as they are doing it at *your* business on *your* business's clock.

According to a study reported at Salary.com, American companies spend more than $750 billion (that's *billion* with a *b*) paying people for work they're *not* doing. Add to that your best guess for the amount paid to people for work they are doing that's not in compliance with the employers' standards, policies, and procedures. Whatever share of that is coming out of your pocket is too much.

In the workplace, "big brother" has to watch. The cat must never be away.

There are several ways to accomplish this.

One is with technology. A technoboob myself, I'll keep this short, sweet, and in plain English. Just know there are plenty of service and software and equipment providers you can find to implement every suggestion I'm about to make, and find them and use them you should.

Specific to computers, you can zip in to any of your employees' computers at any time from any location and monitor what's being done with it at that precise moment in real time. You can also access recorded histories of where the computer's user has traveled, the sites he visited, and the e-mails sent. Such things can even be resurrected after they've been deleted. Better, they can be harvested all day long. Even the most computer illiterate of bosses can accurately track the internet usage in his company by location, by office, by department, by individual employee, by day, by hour, by minute.

Specific to workplaces, you can install video and audio surveillance systems, which can record everything and that you can access from any remote location via your laptop and watch and listen in real time. (I've written more about this in Chapter 14.)

Washington State University researchers found that workers who knew they were being watched got more done, but weren't as happy! Gee, I wonder why. Could it be because they were actually having to—say it with me in unison—W-O-R-K? Well, here's a secret: Your really good, honest, productive employees, few by ratio, hate the bad, dishonest, unproductive slugs. The good ones are thrilled when real enforcement with real teeth occurs. It doesn't make the good ones unhappy. Only the bad ones.

Specific to salespeople, installers, delivery drivers, and the like out in the field, there are GPS tracking devices.

And there's more. The point is, if you choose to, you can know who's doing what, when, where, and how . . . whether or not they're complying with your policies, procedures, sales scripts, installation instructions . . . how they are using your assets and your time minute by minute. If you don't choose to, sorry, but you're a chump.

Another way to watch the mice is with human snooping. There are legendary stories of Martha Stewart suddenly, unexpectedly swooping into a Kmart store to inspect the display of the Martha Stewart-brand merchandise and raising hell if it wasn't done properly. Good for her. But the more practical approach is organized, consistent "mystery shopping."

There are professionals who can mystery shop your stores, offices, practices or showrooms, trade show exhibits, or any other place of business. They'll play prospect and call in, they'll visit, they'll pose as customers and buy. Such services are available simple and cheap, or sophisticated and expensive but worth it. You need to determine what level of expertise is appropriate for your business, how indepth the mystery shopping investigations need to be for your purposes, what the frequency ought to be, and whether you want to have the same experts provide or assist with employee training or just use their findings and do the (constant) training yourself. You need to intelligently assess the values of lost customers to arrive at how much to invest in this. Then you NEED to put a comprehensive, ongoing program in place, integrating your *program* (what's supposed to be done and

Recommended Resource #3

SNOOPS FOR HIRE! I have two different "snoop services" that I work with a lot, which I recommend to my clients. Each offers a slightly different level of service. If you'd like a brief report about them and referral to them, go to www.NoBSBooks.com, click on the "MANAGEMENT BOOK" icon, then click on the "SNOOPS REPORT" icon.

how it's supposed to be done), training, mystery shopping, enforcement, rewards, and firings.

You also need to "raid" your employees' work spaces when they aren't there. At least once a month, invest a Saturday morning in carefully searching some of your employees' work spaces. In doing this myself, I've found hidden, long-overdue work, resumes made on my copier and being sent out with my postage (initiative that surprised me), and unanswered complaints from customers. Others have found much worse. Like the client who discovered he had an extremely sympathetic clerk in his employ, who believed any sob story provided by a customer and was taking customers out of the monthly billing system for months on end but still letting the company fulfill the prescheduled monthly shipments of product—to the tune of $236,700.00 of unprocessed credit card charges. When confronted, she was enraged at the invasion of her privacy! And she made it clear she thought her employer sold overpriced, ineffective goods, he didn't deserve to be making all the money he was making, and she was the victim here, being penalized for being a good person giving these customers a break. The fact that she essentially robbed her employer's son of his college fund notwithstanding.

A third way to keep tabs on things is to let good mice, pardon the pun, rat out the bad mice. At my suggestion, a client of mine with several offices, several stores, and several restaurants set up a toll-free number for employees to rat out underperforming or badly performing employees anonymously and safely. They were promised no attempts would be made to determine who called the number. In just the first six months, reports to this anonymous tip line led to catching one employee stealing merchandise from the store on an almost daily basis, another spitting and even putting dirt from the floor in customers' meals, a receptionist putting all the phones on hold while she—honest to Mick—used a little vibrator to pleasure herself . . . for an hour every day, and finally in this hit parade, a clerical employee who was copying the office's customer and lead files every week and selling them to a competitor for cash. To be fair, the owner had to sort through bogus reports of misconduct left on the recording by spiteful employees just seeking revenge against others for various slights. But what he discovered is that good, honest, hardworking employees deeply resent bad employees' bad behavior, want to see them caught and removed from the workplace, and will eagerly rat 'em out if they can do so in secrecy.

Finally, a fourth strategy is to actually be there and manage your business, these days something of a radical concept. A lot of business owners seem more interested in being on the golf course, at the beach, at home, playing with their kids, hanging out at Starbucks®, and everywhere else but at their business, doing everything else but managing it. Well, I'm all for fun in the sun, and I urge business owners to organize their businesses as servants not masters. I also urge business owners to stay away from the business some of the time, to do important, high-value work—like creating advertising or marketing plans—in a more conducive, interruption- and distraction-free environment. But. A very big *but*. I'll keep saying it over and over and over again: If you insist on having employees at all, then you have to accept the responsibilities that come with them. Leadership, management, AND SUPERVISION. Further, it's impossible to really know what's going on in a business if you're never or rarely there. You just can't beat what Tom Peters called MBWA: management by walking around. Listening in. Joining in and doing. Seeing and being seen.

Michael Gerber, the famous E-Myth guy, says most business owners spend way too much time working *in* their business rather than *on* their business. A decade ago, I agreed with him 100%. Now I don't. His observation is sometimes true. It's a sin many business owners do commit. However, there are just as many who sin by not working in their businesses at all. Some even avoid working in OR on their businesses! Suggestion: if you dislike your business so much or are interested in it so little that you avoid being there, working in it, and working on it, then sell it, give it away, or burn it down. Now not later.

The right balance varies business by business. But as a big-thumb rule, I'd say the ratio ought to be about 75% working on the business, 25% working in the business.

To define, working *on* your business means doing big things, strategic things, creative things. Examples would be developing a new product line's advertising campaign, or attending my kind of mastermind and coaching group meetings for exchange of information and ideas with other carefully chosen entrepreneurs, or plotting preshow, at-show, and postshow marketing strategies related to your industry's annual trade show. Many of these things are often better done away from the office, plant, or store, at home or walking around the zoo.

In means hands on, waist deep in the nitty-gritty of implementation and execution. Examples include face-to-face meetings with individual employees and groups of employees to work on specific projects or problems, taking calls from key clients or vendors, or even actually doing work: serving customers, making sales, stocking shelves, potting plants. In some small businesses, the owner has no reasonable economic option but doing some of the work. In all businesses, it's useful for the owner to at least occasionally do a bit of all the work, so he knows what it takes, can't be easily fooled, and everybody knows he knows. "In" time is also wisely and profitably used for more human snooping too. For example, every owner should randomly and periodically snatch all the incoming mail and open and examine it himself before anybody else gets to it. Same with a day's e-mails. Or randomly take an hour or two to answer the phones and actually hear from customers. This is how you keep tabs on what's really going on. No, actually, this is the only way to keep tabs on what's really going on!

Now that I put it that way, it seems eminently reasonable, doesn't it? Well, it's not going to happen by putting some "success posters" up on the wall, holding hands, singing "kumbaya" together.

The Goals Are . . .

- To have a workplace that is a place of work.
- To have a workplace that is a "productivity only" work place.
- To get a fair, just, full day's work for the agreed upon day's pay. From every employee being paid. Every day.
- To get compliant work, meaning work done as you intend it to be done.
- To quickly and ruthlessly identify, eliminate, and replace those employees who refuse to deliver a fair, just, full day of compliant work every day.
- To effectively support the employees who do deliver a fair, just, full day of compliant work, by not saddling them with also having to pick up the slack of the bad employees.

CHAPTER 14

Out Smoking a Cigarette

Trust. But cut the cards.

—PRESIDENT RONALD REAGAN

In an upscale shopping area near the Outer Banks in Virginia, my colleague Lee Milteer wandered into a luxury women's wear shop—to find it deserted. On the counter, a person's open purse and a cell phone. She called out; she looked in the back room. She shopped for more than ten minutes and did find a couple of things she would have purchased, had there been anyone there to ring up the sales. Periodically, the store's phone rang, 10, 20 rings, and went unanswered. At the 15-minute mark, Lee gave up and left, actually a little worried—had the staff been kidnapped? Were they tied up in the basement?

As she exited, somebody called out to her from across the street. A woman, seated at a patio table with two other women, yelled to her: "Is there something in the store you'd like to see?"

Lee walked over to find the women smoking and drinking coffee. She asked the one who yelled if she was the owner. She said no; she just "ran the place." At which point Lee gave her a brief "motivational" speech: "If I knew the owner, I'd have your posterior fired. You saw me enter the store and still stayed over here smoking. You're so dumb you left your purse, wallet, and cell phone on the counter. And the store's phone has been ringing off the hook. You *need* to be fired."

Odds are, had Lee succumbed to the fleeting temptation to answer the store's phone on the 20th ring, she could have talked to the owner. Later, if the owner asked her employee why she didn't answer the phone, the employee most likely lied and said she was with a customer.

The store lost more than $500.00 in sales. Its owner will never know of the loss. It is just the same as that employee stealing $500.00 in cash from the cash register.

And your immediate response to this is:

Not in MY business.

Not MY employees.

And if that is your reaction, you are either so hopelessly naïve and delusional you need to be put away somewhere safe for your own protection, or you are willfully stupid, to avoid all the ugly work of really, properly managing a business. I find the latter true more often than the former.

It is in damn near EVERY business including yours, and should you care to place a large wager on whether I can catch *your* employees goofing off, driving away customers, ignoring customers, lying and stealing, contact me personally. I like gambling when my win is certain.

This sort of thing is a national epidemic.

Which brings me to my next suggestion.

My Case for Surveillance

My (mostly accurate, yet unwelcome) advice to clients who own stores, restaurants, offices, professional practices, and pretty much any and every kind of business is to install and use full, wall-to-wall video and audio surveillance equipment that can be monitored in real time via a laptop from anywhere. With such a system in place, you can "drop in" many times, at random, from anywhere you may be, without even a warning footstep. Now you can watch and listen to your salesperson's actual sales presentation, watch and listen to the patient being greeted at the counter. In most businesses, it currently costs from $4,000.00 to $10,000.00 to have this sort of system custom installed and internet hosted, and at that, it's the bargain of the century. A small price to give your walls eyes and ears.

This sort of surveillance serves five purposes.

1. Maximum Deterrent Effect

Whenever there's an execution, a bunch of "experts" are trotted out who claim that the death penalty is not a deterrent to criminals. It may not be for people committing crime-of-passion murders. But you'll never convince me that having and promoting the use of the death penalty for an expanded array of heinous crimes and publicly televising the executions wouldn't slow down *somebody.* Professional burglars say that a loudly barking dog is enough to deter them—there are, after all, other houses. Regardless of this theoretical argument, the facts are in regarding workplace surveillance. A number of studies, including one by Washington State University, prove that more work gets done when workers know they are being watched. Years back, when I worked with a top theft control expert in the retail industry, he had a client suffering nearly a 30% employee theft problem in the warehouses. It dropped overnight to under 8% with the installation and monitoring of wall-to-wall video surveillance equipment. I doubt Lee would have found an empty store with its employee parked on her butt at the patio table across the street if said employee knew she and the entire inside of the store were being continuously videotaped and the owner might look in via her laptop at any moment.

2. Employee Security and Legal Liability Protections

You can worry a lot less about sexual harassment or hostile workplace environment litigation if every inch of the workplace is under video and audio surveillance every minute of the time. In a small chain of convenience stores in very bad sections of town, violent acts against employees during robberies dropped from "frequent" to "almost never" as soon as full surveillance systems were installed, were very visible, and signage boldly announced their existence. Unfortunately, the frequency of robberies didn't drop much. But the employees themselves were in less danger.

3. Better Compliance

This is the biggie. If you're a dentist, chiropractor, or cosmetic surgeon, you have a certain way you want the phone answered, a script you want followed when answering callers' questions about fees and other matters, and a prescribed way of greeting people when they enter. But you're in the back drilling teeth or stretching spines or sucking fat out of fannies and installing it in lips, and you can't see or hear what's going on out there. If you own five auto repair shops or oil change shops or tire stores, you have similar procedures for the phone, for greeting customers, for offering upsells ("If we go ahead and change your oil filter now with your oil change, sir, I can give you free windshield wipers"), for shaking hands with customers when they leave. But you own five shops. You can be in only one at a time.

If you own a mail-order company, you have instructed your employees in shipping to pack your packages of whatever carefully, put plenty of bubble pack around them, and fill the carton to the top with packing material so when the top, bottom, or sides of the box get pushed on or have other boxes piled on top in transit, they don't collapse or crumple and wind up with your whatevers getting there all smooshed. You've told them to put your envelope full of bounce-back offers and catalogs inside every box, right on top. But I got a box from you yesterday without enough packing, with the side smashed in, with my whatever smooshed, and no catalog inside. I'm not going to call you up and give you the bad news. It's not my job as a customer to supervise your employees and run your quality control operations. I just won't order from you again. Ah, but if you had a video surveillance system in your shipping room, then you could peek in anytime you liked in real time or pay your son with the MBA you bought who has moved back into the house and is contemplating his navel all day to review the videotapes and give him a $10.00 bonus for each violation he spots and brings to your attention. There won't be as many violations as there most certainly are absent the surveillance equipment, because the folks packing those boxes know they're being watched. If you add audio surveillance, you won't have one sexually harassing the other, or trying to inveigle the other two in a scheme to steal, or trying to talk one of the others into punching his time card for him so he can sneak out early.

Now here's another biggie: These surveillance systems have been relatively common in manufacturing areas, to control theft or foster compliance with health and safety rules. In fast-food restaurants, for example, video surveillance of food prep areas is now common. But, in the future, smart business owners will be using video and audio surveillance to compel compliance by their salespeople with their scripts and prescribed sales practices. This is new. And I am an early screaming advocate and champion.

Years ago, I was hired to do an extensive sales training seminar for a company that owned and operated retirement communities throughout the state of Florida. Beforehand, I did two things. First, I found out how the salespeople were supposed to be selling these properties. Second, I rented a little old lady to playact as my grandmother and went around to the communities to personally experience the sales presentations. I spent two days schlepping my rented grandmother around central Florida. Suffering through the tour by golf cart and sales presentation again and again and again, by different sales reps at each site. Once we saw an alligator at the edge of the golf course lake, and that livened things up a little bit. But guess what we never saw or heard? Right. The sales presentation delivered as it was supposed to be. Not once. Not even close. And a critical "step-down sale technique" crafted personally by the company President, for moving the person not ready to buy a lot down to an open, first right of refusal deposit, and finally to a $250.00 deposit by credit card, was *never* used.

Sure, of course, you fire them all. Or feed 'em to the alligators. But then, what do you replace them with? You just are not going to find a small army of *voluntarily compliant* salespeople. The only way to get compliance is to compel it. I know you instantly think otherwise. You think: *Well, if I show them that my way works best and makes them the most commissions, they'll do it voluntarily.* You're wrong. They won't. They'll think you're a buffoon. They'll freelance. They'll wander off the reservation. You think: *Well, if I tell them it's my way or the highway and I'll fire anybody caught not doing it my way, they'll comply to keep their jobs.* Not a chance unless they are certain they can and will be caught and fired.

What I would advise if I were working with this client today is that every salesperson must bring every prospect into the "closing room" in the office to make the actual presentation, and it be done under video and audio surveillance. In addition, I'd add frequent and random human mystery shopping. But I'd be running *Candid Camera* in there all the time.

4. Better Compliance = Better Profits

Here's the next biggie. Assuming your prescribed sales methods, your telephone and in-person sales scripts, your upsells, your customer service policies, and so on are well designed and profitable if complied with, then better compliance equals more appointments from every *x* number of calls, more closed sales from every *x* number of presentations, happier customers, better retention, more referrals, more orders from catalogs inserted in every well-packed box, lower costs with less waste, and a host of other outcomes that add up to better profits. In fact, the surest and best way to boost profits in your business is to compel compliance with your best practices. This is almost always a greater profit improvement opportunity than any kind of bean-counterish cost cutting. It's usually a better profit improvement opportunity than a sales and marketing breakthrough producing more customers.

5. Personal Freedom

A lot of small-business owners strive for compliance by being on the premises, looking over everybody's shoulders in person. If that's you, my sympathies. Your business has you chained to it, like a big, dumb elephant ankle-chained to a stake driven into the

Recommended Resource #4

The expert I recommend in these kinds of surveillance systems, who understands the purposes for having them described in this Chapter and assists business owners in using them as management tools, is Michael Gravette. At my request, he has established a special informational web site just for readers of this book at: www.SurveillanceManagement.com, or you can communicate with him directly by e-mail: Michael@SurveillanceManagement.com.

ground. You're in prison. Hey, I think your paranoia is well justified; I just think you're treating it with the wrong medicine. Implement a full-scale surveillance program and learn how to use a laptop, and you can oversee your operations from anywhere. You can go somewhere free of interruptions to work *on* your business or spend a pleasant afternoon at the lake on your fishing boat yet still, simultaneously, be supervising *in* your business. You are at once liberated and multiplied.

CHAPTER 15

The Holiday Inn Telephone Warning System

Elementary, my dear Watson!

—The famous quote never actually spoken by Sherlock Holmes in any Arthur Conan Doyle novel or story

For a couple years, during our family's "poor dad years," my father had a second job as a banquet manager, room service guy, and handyman at the local Holiday Inn. Holiday Inn periodically put an executive or team of executives on the road to pull surprise inspections on the Holiday Inns in different areas. Turned out, it wasn't much of a surprise. There were seven Holiday Inns ringing Cleveland at the time. Whichever inn the inspectors arrived at first immediately called the other six to warn them.

Employees often cover for each other. This is how you wind up with the culture of corruption that permeates the U.S. Congress or might infect a police precinct. They're in their own private club. You aren't in their club. Push to shove, they'll side with each other more often than with you. At the very least, they look the other way while those around them behave badly. At worst, they'll be enticed to join in.

I was waiting in the reception area of a professional's office. He comes in and out through the back door. The door inexplicably has a door chime on it, which can be heard whenever it is opened. When it chimed, I watched his front-desk staff put away the Avon catalog, pull up work on the computer, and hastily get very busy. Two minutes later when he arrived at the front of the office to welcome me, his front office was a beehive of important-looking activity. "Looks like they'll need overtime again this week," he said, "just to keep up with everything. I'm advertising right now to add a sixth employee."

I said, "It'd be cheaper to disconnect the door chime."

CHAPTER 16

Thieves Like Us

All the children in Lake Wobegon are above average.

—GARRISON KELLIOR

I learned a lot in the several years I spent working with, then, America's #1 expert in employee and deliveryman theft control in the supermarket, convenience store, and drugstore categories. Virtually every major national and regional supermarket and convenience store chain had him training its managers and providing "human systems," meaning strict procedures to be used in the stores. He knew his stuff in part because he, himself, was a former deliveryman thief who not only had robbed the stores he delivered bread and baked goods to himself but also had collaborated with the stores' employees on much of the theft.

I learned, for example, that there are more than 152 ways that store employees and the deliverymen steal from store owners every single day. I learned that shoplifting is trivial compared with all the internal theft, contrary to what most companies and business owners insist on believing. I learned how to walk into any cashier's area and instantly tell you whether or not she's stealing—and often, how much. I learned how to beat bar codes. I learned how to spot a lot of the deliveryman thieves with one simple observation, from a distance. Mostly, I learned that every business has thieves. (See Recommended Resource #3 in Chapter 13.) But, beyond those specifics, here's how this applies to every single reader of this book with any kind of business and employees.

You will start out vehemently denying it, but you *now* have employee theft occurring in your business. The only questions are type, quantity, and frequency, not if. In all probability, it's a big hole through which your profits are disappearing, which can and should be plugged. It's a way to immediately increase profits without investing a plugged nickel in more advertising, marketing, products, customers, or staff. To begin moving from your vehement denial to plugging your profit holes, we need to recognize that your employees are thieves like us!

Now you're in denial *and insulted*.

Give me five minutes to change your mind, change the way you manage your business and all your relationships forever, and empower you to make a lot more money from now on.

The Secret of Situational Ethics

You are at the grocery store as a customer. You get out to your car and there realize the clerk gave you $8.00 too much in change. Do you go back into the store to return the $8.00? Almost everyone would.

You are at the grocery store, with your twin six-year-old boys, who are overdue for a nap. You parked your car way far away from the busy store. You get out to your car and there realize the clerk gave you $8.00 too much in change. Do you go back into the store to return the $8.00?

You are at the grocery store, with your twin six-year-old boys, who are overdue for a nap. You parked your car way far away from the busy store. It's pouring rain. One of the bags rips as you lift it out of the shopping cart, spilling several items into a puddle. When you finally get into your car, you then realize the clerk gave you $8.00 too much in change. Do you go back into the store to return the $8.00?

You are at the grocery store, with your twin six-year-old boys, who are overdue for a nap. You parked your car way far away from the busy store. It's pouring rain. One of the bags rips as you lift it out of the shopping cart, spilling several items into a puddle. And the cashier was rude to you. And you are already a half hour late getting home to get ready for the twins' birthday party. When you finally get into your car, you then realize the clerk gave you $8.00 too much in change. Do you go back into the store to return the $8.00?

At what point do you begin thinking, "Hey, it's not MY job to count change for her. And eight bucks is no big deal to that store. And geez, I spend a lot of money there, I'm a good customer, I deserve a break."

I'm sure you consider yourself an honest, ethical, moral person, yet in this example, you just stole money and justified it in a way that—until I ruined it—let you continue thinking of yourself as an honest, ethical, moral person. And that's a big part of the problem; anybody can find a way to justify all kinds of really bad behavior without ever looking in the mirror and calling himself a liar, cheat, or thief.

So, here's how humanity divides. There are 5% of the people who are hardwired never to lie, cheat, or steal. They can't. Starving, if they see a loaf of bread fall out of a bread truck, they'll pick it up and chase the truck to give it back. You can try to hire only such people, and, in fact, there are tests predictive of honesty you might want to use in hiring. But the likelihood of you being able to meet all your employee and vendor needs with people in this unique 5% is, well, at best 95-to-5. Terrible odds. These people also tend to be useless in most jobs, because most jobs *require* situational ethics! Your secretary has to lie and say you're out when you're in. Your dental assistant has to pretend to be interested in Mrs. Persimmon's long-winded story of her grandchild's wrapping the neighbor's cat in aluminum foil. Your ad copywriter better use some "poetic license" in romancing whatever stone you sell. Further, these truly sanctimonious, rigid, and unbending saints are no fun to be around.

Oh, and just for the record, there are no obvious guarantees somebody's in this unwaveringly, perfectly honest category. I actually had a client who would hire only professed evangelical Christians who matched his faith, and I observed them stealing him blind. Be a bad idea to rely on religiosity. The Catholic Church's leaders lied and schemed to cover up a massive problem with pedophile priests, then mercilessly stonewalled the victims, then wound up having to steal millions put in collection plates by well-meaning parishioners eager to support the church's "good works" in order to pay off victims and lawyers.

There are technical terms for this: *racketeering* and *organized crime*. Over in the evangelical community, we've had Jim and Tammy Faye blithely selling the same time share for 860% use, and Swaggart, and the guy with the homosexual prostitute. And the happy hit list reaches far back in history and will keep reoccurring in the future. I could go on and insult every organized religion. If yours wasn't named, don't feel smug. The point is this: the badge of spirituality worn on lapel is absolutely not a warranty of good or honest behavior. Be a bad idea to rely on position of trust either—say, lawyers and judges sworn to uphold the law, or elected officials from your local mayor to Presidents of the United States, plural. *"I am not a crook." "I did not have sexual relations with that woman."*

Pretty much anybody who presents himself as being in the 5% who will never lie to you or steal from you is lying. Odds are 95-to-5.

There are also 5% who are hardwired to lie, cheat, and steal at all times, in every situation, even when it doesn't benefit them. They can't NOT steal. They are often detectable with tests and reference checks. However, your odds of encountering such incorrigible characters are also 95-to-5 against.

It's the 90% in between, where you and I live, that causes all the trouble.

For us, there are three things necessary to steal: (1) perceived or real need, (2) ability to rationalize the acts, and (3) belief we can go undetected.

Now we get to the crux of this matter: how you plug the theft holes in your business.

Quickly, we have to define *theft*. In the grocery store there's some obvious theft, like eating food and not paying for it—it's called "grazing." One hundred employees each eat one package of Twinkies®, one bag of chips, one candy bar, and drink one Coke® each day, call that $3.00 hard cost; $300.00 a day; $109,500.00 a year. But at their profit margins, they need to sell about $1,000,000.00 to equal that. So it is like stealing One Million Dollars. Or the bigger, more brazen stealing of steaks to take home. Or 80 or so other thefts. There and in most businesses, there's a lot of known and shrugged-off theft, like running off a kid's homework project on the company copier using a ream of your paper, your toner, your electricity, and a half hour of your paid-for time. Finally, maybe most dangerous, is all the unobvious, nonsanctioned theft, from stealing toilet paper (about which I have an amusing story) to stealing time (a lot; more about this in a minute) to theft by sabotage of your advertising, marketing, and promotions (examples coming up).

There's Only One Way to Plug the Holes

You cannot control somebody's needs or perceived needs. Martha Stewart had no need to make or avoid losing $10,000.00 when she foolishly risked her brand, personal reputation, and entire empire by impulsively engaging in insider trading, then lying about it, then getting nailed for obstruction of justice and being sent to the clink. If you put 100 billionaires in the room and ask how many need more money, all the hands will go up. Whether psychotic need or real need, effect's the same. If you aren't safe with billionaires in your employ (yes, they'd eat the Twinkies® without paying for them too), imagine just how unsafe you are with your people, given the wages you pay and their bad financial habits. A lot of inside theft and embezzlement starts, by the way, when a situationally ethical person is confronted with a new and dramatic ethical dilemma, like discovering her husband has not been making the mortgage payments and now there's $20,000.00 needed in 30 days to avoid foreclosure or getting a call from her favorite grandson, who has just been arrested for driving around with a car full of prescription drugs for which he has no prescriptions and needs $5,000.00 nobody has for a lawyer. The first problem occurs in roughly 1,000 households a week, peaking right around the time the damned Cowboys fail to cover the spread three weeks in a row. The second problem or variation thereof happens with comparable frequency, even in the best of families—think Al Gore's. So, your normally, nearly honest, situationally ethical employee is suddenly faced with a choice: you or her house, you or her grandson. You cannot control need or perceived need with pay, pay raises, bonuses, motivational seminars, best-employee-of-the-month parking spaces, long relationships, membership in the same church. You can NOT.

Next, the ability to rationalize the theft. You cannot control a person's inner thoughts and twisted logic. Consider:

- *There's a room full of copy paper here. What's one ream?*
- *There's a store full of Twinkies® here. What's one package?*
- *I'm stuck here working my ass off while he (the owner) is off cavorting with his girlfriend at the beach hanging with buddies at the golf course/at some trade show in Las Vegas—where I never get to go/etc. and the cheap bastard hasn't given me a raise in a year . . . I deserve this . . .*
- *Suzie, Carol, and Ted are all doing it. Why should I be the only sap?*
- *He charges outrageous fees. He can certainly spare . . .*

You get the idea.

And combining real need with such rationalizations, now you've got something. When I was a young kid, our family was very well off. In my teens, we were very poor. My father went from "rich dad" to "poor dad" almost overnight. For a number of years he worked a number of bad, low-wage jobs, usually two at a time. One was in a window factory, one at a gas station, one at the local Holiday Inn, handling meeting and banquet room setup and room service deliveries. In contrast to where he'd been, it was demeaning and discouraging. But he always did his job well, never shirked, never let his disappointment and frustration adversely affect his work. He was a "good employee." Also, my father was, usually, one of the most honest people ever to walk the planet. He would never dream of actually stealing from anybody. But at this time, we were really, really, really broke and it wasn't a secret. He was driving to work in my beater car I'd bought for $25.00 because his bad car was broken down and needed several hundred dollars of repairs that could not be paid for, and the gas station was already carrying a hefty tab for the gasoline put in the car to get to and from work. So when my father found a big package of frozen hamburgers and box of buns on the seat of his car after work, he asked no questions and brought home what he called his "tip." It was, of course, stolen from the kitchen by the chef and put in the car. And my father was not a stupid man. This occurred not once but with regularity for months. Overall, you couldn't find a better employee than my father. Always there, always on time, competent, pretty good attitude, self-disciplined and requiring little supervision, with a good ethic about quality and getting things done right. However, he was also a co-conspirator in continual theft. It's a safe bet that the charitable chef was putting a few goodies in his own car, too.

My father, of course, had a terrific collection of rationalizations for what was going on that I need not list here. I can remember a dozen or so he voiced when I questioned this. He was poorly paid; the hotel's owner was a big corporation owned by rich people and they would certainly never miss a package of pork chops or ten pounds of beefsteak; his boss was a moron; and so on and so forth, plus the fact that we really, really, really needed the food. And we even shared some of it with a family friend also in dire financial difficulty at the time. Robin Hood.

Truth be told, were you to find yourself in the same circumstances, you would probably behave in exactly the same way. That's important to understand—they are thieves *like us*. Some worse than us, some engaging in theft behavior we would not. But many engaging in theft behavior we would. It's just not as simple as "good people" and "bad people." This has to do with 90% of the people.

OK, so you can't control need and you can't control the ability to rationalize.

That leaves only the thief's belief that he can get away with it undetected. This is the only thing you can control, and control it you must. Unless you're happy seeing your profits carted off by thieves.

In the aforementioned retail categories where my theft control expert client worked, the net profit margins are so thin that the employee and deliveryman thieves combined get a higher percentage of store sales for themselves—with no capital investment, no risk, no leases, no equipment, and, hey, no employees!—than the stores' owners do! Your situation is probably less dramatic. Still, it won't take much theft of cash, goods, time, or sabotage per employee per day to add up to the difference between you retiring wealthy or not. I realize that idea isn't enough to motivate most business owners to do much about this. For some reason, business owners who would be enraged at an employee stealing cash from the register or embezzling from the checking account take a much more casual attitude about all other kinds of theft. So I'll finish with a brief look into the other thefts that might get your blood boiling enough to act.

Here's a great case history. A large tax preparation office's owner devised and ran a big gift-with-appointment promotion. When a new customer came in to meet with the tax preparer, he got to choose a free gift: a set of steak and carving knives, a leather duffel bag, a cubic zirconia tennis bracelet, or a nifty little camera. Each item carried a price tag and retail value of $50.00 to $99.00. And the customer got to enter a drawing for a Las Vegas vacation, where, presumably, he could blow his tax refund. In marketing lingo, that's called a *relevant premium*. Anyway, this business owner spent a lot of his valuable time planning the promotion, writing the ads and newspaper inserts and fliers, placing ads and coordinating the mailing (investment 1). Then he spent about $10,000.00 on advertising space, printing, and postage (investment 2). He also staffed up for the two weeks of the promotion (investment 3). One day he entered his private office through its back door so his receptionist didn't realize he was there and overheard her telling a new customer presenting his coupons:

> *You know this is a scam, don't you? My boss is buying that junk dirt cheap from some closeout place and you're paying for it anyway cuz you can get your tax work done cheaper at H&R Block. And I'm betting a relative wins that trip.*

And off went the customer.

As bad as that is, with freshly motivated investigation, he found seven of his ten tax preparers failing (refusing) to have the "upsell conversations" with the customers about the other financial services offered. One of the preparers was undercharging for work being performed and pocketing $10.00 bills under the table from the customers getting the big discount.

In short, his office was a den of thieves.

Let's say his investments, $10,000.00 in advertising and another $10,000.00 in time, brought in 400 new customers, at a cost of $50.00 each. Harriet The Not-On-Board Receptionist stole $50.00 by driving off that customer, right? Wrong. We don't know how many customers she was telling her truth to, but that number is more than one. Based on the ad results and some snooping, he figured at least 50. Now we're up to $2,500.00. But that doesn't include the lost profits, on their business plus expected referrals of family members and co-workers. And the lost business due to their spreading the word to others. Harriet stole at least $50,000.00. Theft by sabotage.

Incredibly, after confronting her, he defended her to me. *She was having a bad day. She might be right about it being too carnival-like and unprofessional of a promotion. She'd been with him a long time.*

She swore she'd never do it again. Harriet ought to be in sales. She's wasting her talent.

By the way, he earns about $200,000.00 net from his business. She stole 25% of his pay.

Of course you can't imagine this going on in *your* office. Doesn't mean it isn't. Just means you lack imagination.

Doesn't need to be this blatant either. Can just be your grizzled, cynical salesman who poisons the attitudes of your new recruits, telling them you don't know what you're talking about, that your lead generation ads pull in mooches who just want the free stuff and can't be closed, and that using your presentation is a waste of time. He's stealing from you. Could just be your staff person who's supposed to be doing patient recalls on the phone when not needed at the front desk but is, instead, playing on MySpace.com or doing her Christmas shopping at eBay (or running her side business on eBay) and simply falsifying the call reports. She's stealing.

There's only one way to plug all these holes and control all this theft. Here's my theft expert's "cookie lecture":

> *Mom and little Johnny are at home during the day. No one else is there. Mom bakes a dozen fresh chocolate chip cookies. Mom then decides to walk out to the mailbox at the end of the driveway and get the mail. If she expects there to still be a dozen cookies there when she returns, she must call Johnny into the kitchen and say: "Johnny, we are saving these* 12 *cookies until your father gets home. You are not to eat any while I go out to the mailbox, get the mail, and come back. If you do, you will be punished. Now, Johnny, there's no one here but you and me. Not your father. Not the dog. Nobody. You and me.*

Together we will count the cookies—1, 2, 3, 4, 5, 6, 7, 8, 9, 10, 11, and 12. I am now going to the mailbox. You will be the only one here. The minute I get back, you and I will again count the cookies. If there are not 12 there, your ass is grass."

You'd Better Start Counting All the Cookies—and Never Stop

In some cases you must *literally* count the cookies. It's called inventory control. If you're a dentist and you give a tube of special toothpaste and a bottle of mouthwash to every new patient, and you start out on the first of the month with 36 of each in stock, and see 30 new patients, there damn well better be 6 of each left at the end of the month. Instead, most dentists have the same person in charge of inventory control and purchasing all the supplies. She's counting her own cookies. Won't be long before it occurs to her she can take some home with no risk of ever being caught.

In most cases, it's not as simple as actually counting cookies. Time theft and theft by sabotage, trickier. But still manageable. In Chapter 13 I talk about how to control the computers and internet use, use of cell phones with built-in movie, music, text messaging, games, even pornography in the workplace, and time and tasks. I talk about the use of video and audio surveillance as well as human mystery shopping and snooping to detect theft by sabotage and noncompliance. I didn't put that in this book for fun.

I can't end without my toilet paper story. Years ago, I took over an audiocassette production company, manufacturing multi-cassette programs for authors, speakers, consultants, and training companies on sales, management, motivation, and self-improvement topics. We had a large warehouse full of inventory of these products, behind a chain-link wall and a cage door with a giant lock. Anybody going in or out had to get one of the two supervisors with a key to let him through.

After a few months there, I noticed that we were buying truckloads of toilet paper, paper towels, soap, and similar sundries. This was all stored in a closet conveniently near the factory exit, with no lock. I called my plant manager in and said, "I have figured out why our productivity is so low. To use the quantity of toilet paper we are using, every employee is sitting in the bathroom 6.8 hours a day." I told him to take the motivational tapes out of the cage and lock up the toilet paper. There was no risk of the employees stealing self-improvement tapes. But toilet paper—you betcha!

DO YOU PRACTICE

SITUATIONAL ETHICS?

"Honey, does this dress make me look fat?"

CHAPTER 17

Broken Windows, Broken Business

Little hinges swing big doors.

—W. Clement Stone, author of *Success System That Never Fails*

The best, most truthful, most useful business management book I have read—out of more than 300—is Michael Levine's book *Broken Windows, Broken Business,* and I urge getting it, reading it, and taking it seriously. Its core, the so-called "broken windows theory," was first enunciated by two criminologists in a magazine article in 1982. Their idea was that aggressively policing even the pettiest criminal acts, such as graffiti or loitering, could clean up a neighborhood and reduce all crime, because of the message it sent. Conversely, that petty crime ignored equaled broken windows in a building; an invitation to further decay. They said that a building with one broken window left unrepaired would soon have all its windows broken, and a neighborhood with such buildings would soon be consumed by crime and decay. The broken windows communicate that property owners and community leaders do not care. **Little things shrugged off invite anarchy.**

This theory, scoffed at by many in law enforcement, was the basis for Rudy Giuliani's zero tolerance policy for all crime, which led to a true renaissance of New York City while he was mayor. During his tenure, the numbers of murders, assaults, and other violent crimes went down, a generally unlivable city became livable, landmark areas like Times Square went from prostitute and drug dealer territories to welcoming areas for tourists—and it all started with an insistence on cleaning up graffiti on subway cars. The Giuliani cleanup of New York is explained in considerable detail in Levine's book, as the basis for business applications. Levine says that in business,

> *. . . a broken window can be a sloppy counter, a poorly located sale item, a randomly organized menu, or an employee with a bad attitude. It can be physical, like a faded, flaking paint job, or symbolic, like a policy that requires consumers to pay for customer service. When a call for help in assembling a bicycle results in a 20-minute hold on the phone, that's a broken window. When a consumer asks why she can't return her blouse at the counter and is told "Because that's the rule," that's a broken window.*

In short, tiny things sabotage big things. Not long ago I was in a dentist's "Taj Mahal office" with luxury décor throughout, coffee latte and biscotti, a fountain, a floor-to-ceiling aquarium on one wall. Friendly, personable staff in crisp uniforms. Above the dental chair, a 42-inch flat-screen TV. Everything in deliberate harmony with this dentist's positioning as "the best" and his way above average fees. But in the corner of the operatory, just above that TV, a little cobweb. In another corner, wall covering torn and scuffed. And the window was a little dirty. Those three defects stuck in my mind and pushed everything else about the office's designed-to-impress environment out of my mind. I later found myself commenting about the three defects to a friend.

A leading Thoroughbred breeding and boarding farm in Kentucky where, for several years, I had Thoroughbred broodmares has a long, long, long approach road with white three-rail fences on both sides, horses with shiny coats in the pastures. The owners of the farm have full-time employees who do nothing but paint those fences. They start at one end, paint to the other, turn around and paint back in the other direction. Day in, day out. Why? "Because," the owners told me, **"we are judged by our fences."** Implicit in this answer is that it would not matter how good their core services were, how professionally and perfectly they cared for the boarded horses, how many winners their studs begot, if people's perception of the place was "second class." Levine says that perception is something that happens in the blink of an eye. I would add: or in one poorly chosen sentence said, one brusque or rude response, one too-long wait or delay. Any broken window is one broken window too many.

Magnificent Obsession

Simply put, not only do you have to decide to have zero tolerance for broken windows in your business, but you have to be *obsessed* with it. Decide that nothing is insignificant. Nothing is to be shrugged off. Nobody excused from ruining a customer's perceptions of your business as "just having a bad day." Of course, most business owners will insist this is totally unreasonable. After all, who can afford to have somebody doing nothing but painting fences, washing windows, immediately repairing a wallpaper tear, policing the message conveyed by the physical facility? Wrong question. You can't afford not to. That cost is nothing compared with your losses racked up in wasted ad and marketing dollars to bring people through your doors only to leave with a negative impression. But, hey, everybody has a bad day once in a while, right? No such permission can be given. Your people need to show up ready to play, or you'd be better off if they stayed home and had their bad day with only their family as victims. This is all top down, just as it was in New York City. Just as it is for Trump, known for his obsessive-compulsive behavior and temper tantrums over a lone cigarette butt left on the floor of his property's men's room or any other appearance defect. You need to be obsessed, compulsive, eagle-eyed, eagle-eared, intolerant, constantly leading and coaching and disciplining on these issues.

NO B.S. Ruthless Management Truth #5

Any broken window is one too many.

A big part of your "zero tolerance for broken windows policy" must govern your personnel. Again quoting Levine (capitalizing mine): "When an employee—ANY employee—becomes a detriment to the company for ANY reason, that employee has become a broken window, and the ripple effect from his or her FAILURE, however slight, can be DEVESTATING to your business."

What about reasonable tolerance for human frailty, human error, human inconsistency? Levine:

> *There is a significant tendency in business today to forgive more than is rational . . . . Employees, even those on minimum wage, can no longer be allowed to sleepwalk through a day's work when dealing with the clientele. They can't be putting in their time at work and failing to uphold the integrity of the company with each and every encounter they have. They can no longer be allowed to consider their jobs a distraction from their lives . . . . businesses these days are far too slow to fire people. More employees should be getting fired. Often they should be fired immediately. Why? Because they are not performing the jobs for which they were hired in the first place.*

Amen, brother.

Recommended Resource #5

Michael Levine is the author of 17 business books including *Broken Windows, Broken Business*, which I highly recommend. You can learn more about him at www.LCOonline.com or www.BrokenWindows.com.

A Word about Moral Authority

Years ago, I did a favor for a client, a doctor with a large chiropractic clinic. He was frustrated by his employees routinely arriving late for work, returning tardy from lunch, and, to use Levine's term, sleepwalking through their jobs on Mondays and Fridays. He asked me to come in and conduct a little class on "peak personal productivity," with the secret intent of encouraging more responsible behavior. My little class was scheduled for 9:00 A.M. to 11:00 A.M. on a Saturday, to be followed by a light lunch. He was to pick me up at the hotel close to his office at 8:30 A.M. He arrived at 9:05 A.M.—with me standing outside, fuming. We got to his office at 9:20 A.M. I did not give the presentation he'd asked for or expected. I did "Dan lite" and entertained them. Afterward I told him that I had diagnosed the real problem and it wasn't his staff, and that neither he nor I by proxy had any moral authority for a lecture on time management and responsible behavior. He was his own broken window.

CHAPTER 18

On the Other Hand, Good Enough Is Good Enough

The physician can bury his mistakes but the architect can only advise his client to plant vines.

—Frank Lloyd Wright

I am constantly haranguing my clients not to be perfectionists. Perfectionism is paralysis. Perfectionism is costly. Perfectionism is a distraction from the reality of winning and losing in business. It is often promoted in management books and seminars as some sort of holy grail to endlessly pursue, yet it's the wrong mission altogether if our chief goal is maximum profit.

I'm a huge believer in "good enough is good enough." I personally practice it to the greatest extent possible. For example, this book will have been picked at by editors and proofreaders over months, attempting to force me into perfect grammar and syntax, doing battle over politically incorrect and insensitive statements that might offend even one easily offended pygmy, and, of course, striving for certain prevention of even one typographical error. Consequently, it takes six months to a year for this publisher and most traditional publishers to get a book to the shelf after it's been written. In my own businesses, I write five newsletters each month, several books each year, a weekly fax, and dozens of home study courses every year, and I shove them all out the door so full of typographical and grammatical errors they can keep a widowed, sexless schoolmarm occupied for months on end. That flawed product output satisfies well over 100,000 happy, repeat, frequent customers and fuels a thriving business that includes the largest circulation and fastest-growing paid subscription newsletter of its kind. It also facilitates rapid speed to market. But how can all this flawed output be so wildly successful? Because its consumers care far, far more about the value of my advice, my prolific output, and my speed of providing it to them than they do about dotted *i*'s and crossed *t*'s. And because I deliberately attract such sane customers. And because I manage their expectations carefully and overdeliver against what's promised and expected. (Not against some false god of perfection. Against what's promised and expected.) For me and for them, my good enough is more than good enough!

So, there is no existential conflict between the "no broken windows allowed" and "good enough is good enough" concepts. None at all. They're perfectly compatible. The bridge between the two is "standards."

Establish the Best Standards for <u>Your</u> Business

General Norman Schwarzkopf, who brilliantly prosecuted Gulf War I to a quick and successful conclusion, appeared immediately before me as a speaker on about 30 or 40 large public seminar events over a period of two years. We waited in the Green Room backstage together for an hour or so on each of those occasions, so we got to know each other reasonably well. My take on Schwarzkopf is that what you see is what you get, no pretending. So his speech about leadership given by his onstage persona accurately reflected how he actually led his troops offstage and out of sight of any audience. And unlike most of the nincompoops writing books about leadership, he actually practiced his principles in real-life situations. In his speech he pointed out that, in most cases, if people screw up in business, only money is lost, but out there on the battlefield, lives are lost. He said the key to keeping as many people alive as possible while successfully waging and winning war was "standards." When I asked him about his comments privately, he said that nuances are nice for whiskey and cigar conversation and flexibility is a synonym for enough rope to hang yourself with. In battlefield conditions it is most useful for everyone to have been brought up on and conditioned to perform within absolutely rigid standards. It is my contention that the very same thing is true in business. Casual can get you killed.

Only you (and your customers) can decide what your standards should be, to facilitate your optimum success in the marketplace. But decide you should.

Consider the food service business. McDonald's® has a vast, successful, even dominant empire built on the solid foundation of *mediocre* food. Everybody with the brain of a flea, the life experience of a ten-year-old, and any taste buds at all knows full well there are better-tasting burgers readily accessible to them at any number of places. It's not a secret. The standards that McDonald's®

and its customers have wound up in agreement on have to do with consistent and reliable mediocre quality, cheap prices, and fast service. For McDonald's® to invest time or money in making its burgers taste better or taste fresher would be a giant waste and a form of perfectionism as paralysis. Doing so would undoubtedly raise prices or slow service and would likely never be appropriately rewarded. However, the Palm® or Smith and Wollensky™ steakhouses have very different covenants with their customers and must meet much more exacting standards concerning food excellence, although slow service is not a problem. The servers have to be knowledgeable, friendly, conversational, and attentive, but *slow* service is expected. Oh, and these places are noisier than hell, and that's expected too. (If you want quiet, you go to Flemings®.) We can go through the restaurant industry chain by chain, Starbucks®, Dunkin' Donuts®, Denny's®, Domino's®, on and on. Each has a different covenant with its customers mandating certain standards. In very few cases are those standards "perfect" or even "excellent" in every category of fulfillment. And achieving "excellent" in ways outside the covenant would rarely be financially rewarding. However, failing to meet the standards dictated by the particular business's covenant with its customers, in even the tiniest of broken-window ways, will very, very quickly rot and ruin the business.

Finding the Magic GE-Spot

What I'm about to describe is enormously rewarding and admittedly difficult, but finding the GE-Spot isn't half as maddening as trying to find the G-spot!

The GE-Spot is "the Good Enough Spot."

Your leadership role here is to figure out exactly what your customers value most vs. what they value least in a relationship with a business like yours. Not what's important to you. Not what you think *should* be important to them. What IS important to them. To figure out what aspects of your business offer opportunity to "wow" your customers and give you some sort of competitive advantage—without undue cost, without the paralysis of perfectionism. To be able to communicate this clearly to others.

You must arrive at a comprehensive understanding of the "Good Enough Spot" in every aspect of your business. Determining this is magic of the highest order. This is how you finally quantify what so few business owners can ever quantify. How you clear away the fog of uncertainty, confusion, and vague ideas from your own thinking, your employees', your suppliers', and your customers'. Having a clear and definitive "Good Enough Spot" for every aspect of your business is *the* most empowering management breakthrough possible—and itself worth 100,000 times the little price paid for this book.

To be sure I've conveyed this accurately, consider these examples of the "Good Enough Spot" concerning when and how quickly the telephone is answered in a business. For the criminal defense attorney, bail bondsman, or "fixer-type" publicist serving celebrity clients, the GE-Spot is probably 24/7, first ring. For the flower shop, it might be 9:00 to 5:00, five days a week, third or fourth ring OK, except on the two days immediately prior to and the day of a major holiday like Mother's Day or Valentine's Day, when it probably should be 7:00 A.M. to 7:00 P.M., first ring. For a service business that gets a lot of its business from Yellow Pages ads, like plumbers or chiropractors, we have ironclad empirical evidence that huge, invisible losses are suffered when businesses don't answer 24/7, third ring or faster—consumers with immediate need or interest will not leave messages and wait; they'll just call the next ad and the next until they reach somebody. (Switching these office phones to staff members' cell phones in rotation or to an outside "live" answering service equipped with good scripts and the ability to set appointments or at least guarantee return calls within a set time has proven to be immensely profitable vs. voice mail. And many of these kinds of offices have their phones going to voice mail 30% of the time during regular business hours plus off hours.) Businesses that get their clients by direct-marketing means, establish themselves as expert providers, and offer services purchased more deliberately, such as financial advisory practices, can typically operate successfully with no "live" answering of phones at all; messages invited with a promised and kept time frame for response are sufficient. At my office, we haven't taken incoming calls for years and I'm never accessible to clients or prospective clients without a prescheduled telephone appointment, often after a two- to three-week wait. At the Glazer-Kennedy Insider's Circle™ offices, the customers have been trained to communicate predominantly by fax and e-mail, and, if calling, do not get "live" answering. As you can see, every business's GE-Spot regarding the telephone is located in a different place! So it is with *every* GE-Spot.

It is up to you to locate these GE-Spots and assemble them into a list of specifics that supports the overall positioning of your business.

Your marketing role is to turn that into a clear, clearly understood and embraced covenant with your customers. Your positioning, advertising, marketing, public relations, publicity, sales, physical environments—your entire presentation of your business to the marketplace—have to manage customers' expectations.

A very visible secret about companies that really prosper is that they have clearly understood covenants with their customers. Southwest Airlines® is a great example. I'd describe its covenant as no food, no frills, kind of an ugly boarding process, if you're not early you're probably stuck in a middle seat; basically a bus on wings, but we're kicking butt to take off on time, get you there on time, and our people will ease your pain with good humor. Disney's theme parks' covenant is Walt's original "The Happiest Place on Earth®." There's something going on constantly to make everybody happy. Characters signing autographs, parades, happy music, and every employee—right down to the store clerks trading collectible pins with kids and the street sweepers who initiate helpful conversation with anybody looking confused—authorized and empowered to turn unhappy folks into happy folks by instantly making things right. The last time I was there, I saw a little kid who was waiting in line to see Pluto drop his ice-cream bar on the ground and burst into tears. A Disney employee rushed over, told the kid to wait and he'd bring him a new one, rushed off to the ice-cream stand, and returned with a new ice-cream bar. Each highly successful company has a different kind of clearly understood covenant with its customers. The people running the company and the customers all know where the business's GE-Spot is. They share a common understanding.

Your management role is to translate that covenant into clearly defined standards for how your business operates, how your products are made, packaged, and delivered, how your employees perform, how your salespeople sell. You need to come to grips with both the need to meet your standards 100% of the time without fail, without deviation, and your need not to waste time, energy, or money in seeking perfectionism or excellence outside or beyond those standards. I know, I know, this contradicts so much of what you read and hear from all the happy-thought theorists in creativity, leadership, and excellence bailiwicks. The most famous of all "excellence books" featured companies that went bankrupt or were otherwise marketplace losers in the years following its glorification of them, in part because these companies wasted resources pursuing, and in some cases achieving, celebrated standards of excellence incongruent with their covenant with their customers and their customers' prime directives, at high cost, with poor reward from the investments. Aspiring to unmitigated excellence is a lovely theory. But the reality is that all the most successful, sustained successful, dominant and profitable companies in every category of goods or services find their way to the place I've described. They establish a complex matrix of exact standards and meet them. They don't bother trying to "outexcel" the standards they've established. If you will now examine and analyze highly successful companies through this prism, you'll quickly see just how right I am.

Finally, your supervisory role is to enforce your standards. No exceptions, no excuses, no creative deviation, no improv. And I mean "enforce" in every sense of the word. Not just teach (although you must teach), not just reward (although you must reward). Enforce.

This is the responsibility nobody likes; just about everybody neglects it and desperately rationalizes the neglect, ardently defends the neglect.

Unfortunately, there is more b.s. in management theory books and promulgated by lecturers about this than any other of the responsibilities of business ownership. Combined, it delivers a giant guilt trip. There's the "if you don't trust your people, how do you expect them to trust you," the "you can't run a business like a prison," the "these are old, outdated ideas that won't work with the new worker," and another hundred or more anti-enforcement themes woven through the books, the articles, the seminars. For the business owner already uncomfortable with police work, desperate to be liked, deluded about the actual nature of employer-employee relationships, and eager to avoid enforcement, this blather is cocaine. And it is at least as dangerous.

The problem is, *everything* else you might do right and get right is sabotaged by lack of supervision and enforcement. Every investment you make reduced in value. Every customer you acquire at constant, high risk of loss. Every grand idea, every noble policy, every clever marketing strategy castrated.

FIGURE 18.1: The Four Responsibilities of Business Owners in Dealing with Employees

<table>
<tr>
<td>

Leadership (Motivation)
- 1, 3, 5, 10 Year
- Big Ideas
- Visionary Viewpoints—seeing what others can't yet see
- Defining Purpose, Mission—"What is this business *about*?"
- Setting Major Objectives and Directions—never losing sight of the profit imperative
- Influencing Culture:
  - by example and moral authority
  - by strategic plans

</td>
<td>

Management (Implementation)
- Year, Quarter, Month
- Translating the Big Ideas into:
  - Practical action plans and projects—including plans designed to ensure maximum profit
  - Assembling and allocating resources to support plans
  - The Program—how things are supposed to be done around here
  - Incentive, recognition, reward, enforcement, and punishment policies
  - Measurement and accountability systems
- Integrating the Program with the Promises Made by Marketing
- SERVING Marketing in Every Way Possible

</td>
</tr>
<tr>
<td>

Supervision (Enforcement)
- Minute, Hour, Day, Week; Individual Acts
- Police Work
- Getting Compliance with the Program
- ESPECIALLY Getting Compliance with the Marketing-to-Sales Program
- Police Work
- Disciplining and, when Necessary, Eliminating the Noncompliant
- Police Work
- Making the Trains Run on Time
- Police Work
- Creating an Environment Supportive of Maximum Productivity
- Police Work
- Meeting Profit Targets

</td>
<td>

Marketing (Customer Acquisition, Value Optimization, Retention)
- Years, Year, Quarter, Month, Week, Day/Campaign, Project, Event
- Translating the Big Ideas into a "Position" in the Marketplace
- Leveraging What the Business Does Best into Covenants with Customers
- Attracting Customers Most Appropriate and Most Profitable for the Business
- Repelling Customers Inappropriate and Least Profitable for the Business
- Seamlessly Integrating Advertising, Marketing, Sales and Fulfillment
- Integration with MANAGEMENT and SUPERVISION to Successfully Honor Covenants with Customers

</td>
</tr>
</table>

CHAPTER 19

"But My Business Is Different . . ."

Thought for the Day:
Every morning, all the stupid people you know get together and plan ways to make your life more difficult.

Everybody has some excuse for being unable to manage properly for profit as we're discussing in this book or for being unable to use the highly effective marketing strategies I discuss in the other books in the No B.S. series. Their letting-themselves-off-the-hook escape route from reality often starts with "I totally agree with you" and always features "but my business is different."

I hear this so often it's become an inside joke with my private clients and the business owners in my coaching groups and attending my seminars. One client presented me with a big yellow banner with the five dumb words on it, to hang up in my conference room.

There are just two things you need to know about this.

One: No, it's not.
Your business isn't different.
Nor is anybody else's.

All businesses succeed or fail, prosper or struggle based on the same short list of critical factors. The only possible exception lies within companies that make and sell things only for and to the U.S. government. They can make billion-dollar space shuttles that have to be repaired by spacewalking astronauts with staple guns and duct tape and still get paid in full with our tax dollars. But excepting them, all—repeat: *all*—other businesses win or lose based on executing or failing to execute the same basic game plans. The sooner you get over the limiting and erroneous belief that your business is different, the sooner you'll be able to "borrow" best practices wherever you find them, from diverse businesses outside your own tiny little world, and use them to improve your business. This gives you a big competitive edge because all your competitors have the same narrow perspective. When you broaden yours, you can see what they can't, embrace what they automatically reject, and improve in ways they bar themselves from using.

Two: People who are good at making excuses are never very good at making money.

The two skill sets are in mortal conflict. The "but my business is different" whine is nothing more or less than an excuse for lazily staying stuck with the status quo. No matter how bitterly you complain about it, you are the one unwilling to change it, so shut up. As a matter of fact, if you happen to be dissatisfied with your

NO B.S. Ruthless Management Truth #6

Excuses and profits are incompatible.

income, you might investigate all the excuses you own. People in poverty usually have a wealth of excuses.

As an aside, this is first about you, but then it is also about the people around you—your associates, your employees, and your vendors. Having people around you who are good at making excuses for themselves or for others creates an entire culture of missed deadlines, unkept promises, lost customers, missed sales, waste and inefficiency. At the end of each game, there is a winner and there is a loser. The score is posted on the scoreboard. The list of losers' excuses is never put up there in lights next to the score. There's a reason for that—it doesn't matter. That's the culture you need in your business.

CHAPTER 20

How to Manage at the Speed of Now and Beyond

By Dr. Charles W. Martin, DDS, MAGD, DICOI, FIADFE

If you're going to have a business that involves more than you, you're automatically required to lead and manage that group of people. Even if it's just one other person, you still have to have your own well-defined approach to management and leadership skills.

People are either your greatest asset or your greatest liability. Having *key* people on board with you working with your purposes in mind, understanding your vision, and putting their own energy and sweat and passion into those purposes makes all the difference between success and failure.

Figure 20.1 is a graphic of the Leadership Matrix Cycle I use in my businesses and teach to my clients. Whether you run a solo

FIGURE 20.1: Leadership Matrix Cycle

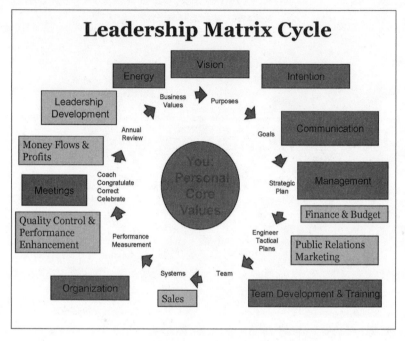

business or one with a large staff, this illustrates the components of success.

Personal Clarity

You'll notice that the middle of the matrix is *you*, what your *personal core values* are. Frankly, if your personal core values are not known and understood, you can't reasonably expect the people around you to act in conformance with them, can you? No one should be asked to be a mind reader.

Out of your personal core values come your business values, and out of both of these stems much of the *energy* that you bring as you create the business that you're in. ***Every day you are creating the business you're in.*** Clarity is critical.

What You See Is What You Get

A business starts as an idea, and this idea must be created with certain parts and pieces. This is called the *vision thing*—you know, vision: the thing that everybody talks about but so few business owners are able to translate into practical actions.

Vision literally means to see. What do you see in your imagination for your future? If you are one that has difficulty imagining the future you want in your mind's eye, talk about it to yourself to describe it, silently or out loud; preferably, record these thoughts. Another way is to feel the future you want. Describe the feelings you want to experience in your future in regard to your business or organization. Make a list of these and then figure out what will have to happen to get those. With both alternatives, form the picture of the future that reflects those words or feelings. Any vision can be made more clear employing both of these techniques.

It is vital to understand that **the clarity of your goals** helps define the **strength and depth of energy** you will have available for their accomplishment. Fuzzy won't cut it.

Making Your Picture Happen

Many business owners fail to get what they picture because they insist on treating their businesses like jobs. ***A job is something***

you work at doing. A business is something you work at creating. To be highly successful requires you to be working *on* your business, not *in* your business. That's a big difference.

Of course, when anyone starts a business, he's working in his business. But ***the moment that you get mired in doing the work*** of your business, you at once limit the size of your business and also limit your ability to move away from it, because you've actually created your own job without the fringe benefits and vacations.

Once you have your picture, values, and goals and you've stated them, now you begin to *communicate* them. In fact, the first person you communicate with is yourself, and then the people around you who need to understand what the goals are. This is part of leadership: to point which way to go and then influence others to go there.

Strategy

We have goals. We communicate these goals to both ourselves and the people around us. Business goals should be communicated and *promoted* to your group to get their buy-in.

You will also create a strategic plan to work toward the accomplishment of these goals. A strategic plan is the broad, general outline of how you're going to accomplish something. It does not have a lot of details in it. It generally runs one to two pages.

It is important to note that many businesses fail at this place. They have no strategy that differentiates themselves from anyone else, and they become just another printer, publisher, lawyer, dentist, butcher, baker, candlestick maker; you name it. They just become *another* one.

So, inherent in your strategy should be: "What is different about us? How are we unique? What plays to our strengths? How are our customers/clients/patients/patrons/members—the people who are going to buy our services or products—going to appreciate who we are and what we offer? How can we use this strategically to get ahead?" Warning: If you said quality or caring about your customer, good luck! Everyone says that, so it has no power to influence. These things matter but are taken as givens in our heavily marketed society.

The strategic plan is where *management* really starts to get involved, because your strategic plan is going to be executed by your people.

Now we have our strategic plan, and it's up to the management to get this strategic plan implemented. It is at this point that we bridge the gap between leadership and management. In actuality, if you have someone who is your chief of operations, his job should be working with you as the leader of the group to **engineer tactical plans out of the strategy**. Ensure that the tactics used to execute the strategic plan are feasible with present resources: that can work, that can be done, that can be used, and that advance you toward your goals. This sounds self-evident, yet many companies take on enormous debt and acquire resources they can't yet afford in trying to accomplish a strategy. This mistake most often leads to insolvency and bankruptcy.

If the tactical plan doesn't mirror the general intent of the strategic plan, it'll be just a bunch of projects, a bunch of things to do, and really won't move you forward at all. Unfortunately, this is the common state of most businesses, small and large.

Worse is a tactical plan that runs counter to your strategic plan. This does happen. For example, I work with dentists on a regular basis, trying to position them in their respective communities as *the doctor* to go to for complex dental problems, the ones that one patient described as "a dental disaster." Advanced training, talent, and skills are required to complete the needed complex dentistry. If the client dentist executes a tactical plan that basically invites every possible patient into that practice, he has just worked against himself. In reality, the doctor wants a specific type of patient for a very specific type of reason, and that's the person the doctor should be focusing on.

Tactical plans include all areas of operations that you have, which include

1. your public relations
2. your marketing
3. your staffing
4. your finance
5. your sales
6. how you're organized
7. your quality control and performance enhancements
8. how you have your meetings and how often
9. how money flows in or out of your business

Tactical plans are going to have a great deal of effect on all of the above.

Next, basic decisions of tactics include

1. Who's going to do it?
2. What authority does the person in charge of the task have?
3. How much money is available to execute the tactic?
4. When does it need to be done by?
5. How is the person in charge going to be measured—what is the definition of a successful result?

These are simple questions that must be answered . . . and often are not!

Profit

A business is living and breathing to the degree that it generates income in a positive way. You need to know how much *profit* you'll produce in an average given day, given a certain level of output.

A standing evaluation I make is to **constantly be thinking in terms of increasing the income-producing work time**. What work can I delegate? What can I eliminate? What can be simplified? What can be outsourced? What could be brought into the business (in-sourced)? It has suited me well, as my practice is four times the size of the average dental practice and I take ten weeks off a year and run four other businesses. It is what I teach my clients, too.

DR. CHARLES W. MARTIN is the founder of Affluent Practice Systems. If you want more information about Dr. Martin's programs, call toll free (866) 263-5577 or go to www.AffluentPracticeSystems.com. His practice web site is www.RichmondSmileCenter.com.

CHAPTER 21

How to Make Every Employee's Job a Profit Center

There are two ways of making yourself stand out . . . one is by having a job so big you can go home before the bell rings if you want to. The other is by finding so much to do that you must stay after the others have gone. The one who enjoys the former once took advantage of the latter.

—HENRY FORD

Susan has to answer the phone. You have to have your phone answered. But what can Susan do while answering the phone to convert that required cost of doing business to a profitable opportunity?

She could ask a few survey questions to collect information, permitting better segmentation of your list. She could tell everybody about your special of the month or direct them to your web site for the article of the week. If taking orders, she can upsell and cross-sell. If taking calls from prospects, she can capture full and complete contact information, for follow-up and to build your mailing list. She can do more than answer the phone.

In your hotel, the maids have to clean the rooms. But they can also place your product catalog in a very visible place (as is done in Westin® properties). She can have a scripted conversation with any guests she encounters in person, inviting them to the hotel's sports bar that night for the big game and free appetizers.

At your restaurant, the waitstaff sell food and beverages, take orders, deliver meals. But they can conversationally urge customers to join the birthday club or VIP club, get those cards filled out. (There is no more valuable asset a restaurant can own than a customer list with birthdays.)

In a dental office, dental hygienists can deliver hygiene. Or they can be taught, coached, and supervised to sell dentistry while delivering hygiene. The difference to a dental practice can be a cost of about $40,000.00 a year to create a terrific profit center worth more than $100,000.00 a year.

Everything I've named so far can be quantified, measured, and, if you choose, incentivized and rewarded. Which I encourage. I like to see every employee have some opportunity to earn bonus money above base pay, at least, based on behavior, but at best, connected to their direct contribution to profits.

One of the greatest breakthroughs that can ever occur in a business is the realization by everyone involved that everything is marketing, and that everyone ought to be involved in marketing. There's a natural inclination to separate "marketing" from "operations," which leads inevitably to viewing some jobs and the employees who perform them as costs, and as necessary evils, rather than as profit centers and opportunities.

CHAPTER 22

Create Better Jobs So You Can Demand More (and Fire Faster)

Companies that grow people, grow profits. Companies that shrink people, shrink profits . . . . Look at the investment in human assets to make sure it's enough.

—TOM CONNELLAN, *INSIDE THE MAGIC KINGDOM*

Make all your important jobs better jobs. Make every position that involves any contact with your customers at all a really, really good job. Pay better than average wages; pay to have employees' uniforms cleaned for them; provide a good working environment; offer significant behavior-, performance-, and results-based bonuses as well as spontaneous, unexpected, varied rewards and recognition. Create jobs people really want and that good people won't want to lose.

Why should you do all this?

Not to be a generous soul. Not to be liked. Not to win some award.

So that your bloody axe is feared and you can be fearless in swinging it.

CHAPTER 23

Exceptions to All the Rules

Never eat at a place called Mom's. Never play cards with a man called Doc. Never go to bed with a woman whose troubles are greater than your own.

—NELSON ALGREN, NOVELIST

If only I'd been given those rules when I was starting out in life!

—DAN KENNEDY

Anybody who has very many employees pass through his portals over time will have a few truly exceptional people—usually they come and go, but sometimes they stay.

One of my clients has five inside sales positions he must keep filled with profitable employees at all times. One woman has been there, in her position, for nearly ten years. She is extraordinary. She loves her job. She likes the high income. She appreciates her autonomy, flexible hours, nominal supervision, and ability to schedule her own vacation time. She meets or exceeds the minimum quota necessary for her to be profitable 100% of the time.

And she cheerfully chips in from time to time to help train the new ones going in and out of the other four chairs at a speed close to that of Ex-Lax® through a diarrheic duck. To keep the other four positions functioning, each at about 70% of the profit she produces, requires hiring and having quit or firing 16 to 24 reps a year. A revolving door. This with extensive work on my part devising a recruiting system to find clones of her, not just doing ordinary "sales help wanted" activity, and using two highly respected hiring assessment tools in the interviewing process. My client suffers slumps in profitability from time to time because he wearies of the revolving-door hiring and firing task, but there's no solution to it. It is what it is. And to make the several-million-dollar-a-year net income he makes from his business, it's an acceptable "ugly"—because no exceptionally profitable business is ever entirely free of "uglies." His management job is as much about managing his own emotions about this "ugly" as it is about managing these people. The exceptional one needs virtually no management. The other four aren't around long enough to manage.

Personally, in my entire career, I believe I've gone through a grand total of 56 or 57 employees in different types of jobs and positions of importance. I have employed family at different times, and my mother and my father were both exceptional employees. Not perfect, mind you; *exceptional* is not a synonym for *perfect*. Exceptional really means more profitable and less troublesome than others you've had in the same position. It's a comparative term, not a definitive one. Anyway, my wife ran my office for a number of years and was exceptional. And I'm fortunate to now be in the fifth or sixth year with my current single employee, personal assistant, office manager, majordomo, and so forth, running my little office all by herself at the opposite end of the country from my two homes. I never go there. We communicate by fax and a brief phone call three times a week, and every Friday I receive a nicely organized big box of bills to pay, mail, faxes, notes for upcoming coaching calls or meetings, checks received, etc. She is exceptional. As is the arrangement, as it violates a number of strong recommendations made in this book, notably making sure to have more than one of everything. I, however, am cross-trained, and my own business is these days a very, very simple one. Glazer-Kennedy Insider's Circle™ is another story altogether, with 19 employees, two office buildings in Baltimore, and a V.P. of Operations reporting to Bill Glazer. I visit there but once a year and have regularly scheduled calls with Bill but am divorced from all management matters.

Two other exceptional-in-their-own-way employees I had working for me for a handful of years were a Hispanic husband and wife. At the manufacturing company where I first had them as employees, they were a problem—they simply could not get to work on time even for a few days in a row. He had nonexistent communication skills, was uncomfortable around people. In these and other ways, they were a disruption to the orderly way that army needed to run. When I left that company, I took them with me to my newer, smaller, leaner business and struck a new deal with them: salary rather than hourly wages, no time clock, a work space all theirs alone to do with as they saw fit, and only one imperative: the required work had to be done and every order fulfilled and shipped by the end of each week. Some weeks they might work a lot, other weeks little. They outfitted their space with a refrigerator and microwave, she brought food and cooked meals. Some days they were invisible but came in at night, with their young toddler, and worked to the wee hours. Essentially, they job shared. I paid them above average wages and left them alone. They were happy and performed. In reality, it was a thin line away from outsourcing. The important thing is that it worked.

Often, working with my clients, I find that when they do wind up with a truly exceptional person, they need to make exceptional (i.e., out of the ordinary) arrangements to keep that person. When they can be, why not make them? I could not have let that Hispanic couple function as they did in a bigger operation with 40 other employees. But in my smaller business, I could, I did, and I'd do it again in a heartbeat.

I do not believe in equality at all. Paying by the job is about the only way you can handle ordinary, commoditized jobs and a bevy of people doing them. At the factory-job level, you're forced into universal pay, universal incentives. But with more important jobs and exceptional people, it's better to structure the job and the compensation to fit the person. Sometimes force fitting an exceptional person into a "hole" drilled out for ordinary people either ruins or drives off the exceptional person, who could be the most profitable person you ever had.

CHAPTER 24

Fairness Be Damned

All animals are equal.
Some are more equal than others.

—George Orwell, *Animal Farm*

Two-time Super Bowl coach Jimmy Johnson told me this: "If Emmitt Smith puts his head down on his desk and dozes off in a team meeting, we get him a pillow and have somebody stand next to him, to be sure he doesn't fall out of his chair if he wakes up suddenly. If a third-string lineman who missed four blocks in last week's game dozes off, he wakes up traded to Buffalo."

CHAPTER 25

To the Winners, the Spoils

REGULATION #5: You are entitled to food, clothing, shelter and medical attention. Anything else you get is a privilege.

—INSTITUTION RULES AND REGULATIONS, ALCATRAZ

Lest you think I'm some sort of Snidely Whiplash character, a boss with a whip and a chair, a trapdoor in front of my desk to drop the out-of-favor employee through to hungry sharks below, there's another side to me and my belief system about managing people for profit. That side is as generous as ol' Saint Nick with the good little boys and girls. I believe in big stockings overflowing with toys. I also believe in lumps of coal.

There's a very good restaurant near one of my homes in northeastern Ohio, in a semirural area between two cities. Its manager conducts a training class for waitstaff titled "How to

Make $100,000.00 a Year Here," and she fully expects her full-time waitpersons to break six figures. The owner wants the top-performing people to enjoy top pay. That sums up my idea of how things ought to work in any business. Employees who excel should have an opportunity to outearn less-effective employees and to earn considerably more than employees in comparable jobs in comparable businesses. You should be the highest-paying employer of your kind to top-performing people.

Years ago, one of the chiropractors attending my marketing seminars for that profession leased shiny new convertibles for each of his five staff people. The cars were theirs to drive as their own, free, as long as they met their described job performance standards and referred two new patients a month in from outside the clinic, from their own circles of influence. From his standpoint, that would guarantee at least ten new patients a month at a lower cost than he could get them from advertising, and he correctly believed that a staff person who wasn't enthusiastic and articulate enough about his practice to bring in two patients a month from all her friends, neighbors, acquaintances, and family shouldn't be let loose talking to his patients in the clinic either. He also presumed this would boost staff morale. And he gave them a grace period of one month per half year when they could miss quota without losing the car. Fail any two months out of six, and you lost the car for six before you could get it back. The idea's brilliant and the results are instructive.

One of the five staff persons loved this deal, never missed a month, usually brought in more than two patients, and was terrific in the office as well. She was appreciative of her nifty little convertible, cheerful, happy to take on extra work, and always supportive of anything the doctor wanted to do to promote his practice. Two met the minimum consistently and were satisfactory employees in every respect. A fourth hung on by a thread. She was still late getting to work from time to time (a failure in meeting minimum standards), and over three years I know of, she lost the car and got it back twice. She was often grumpy and barely worth having in the office. Finally she quit. The fifth lost the car immediately and was underperforming in every other way, and as soon as she lost the car, she became bitter, irritable, and uncooperative and had to be fired. So it all worked out perfectly. It forced him to fire the bottom 20% (one out of five) again and again and again, every 6 to 12 months like clockwork. It caused the next worst to quit. And it rewarded the best performers.

At a simpler level, when I took over a very troubled company with 47 employees, the absenteeism and tardiness stats among the factory and clerical workers were high comedy. I instituted a very simple bonus plan, featuring $100.00 a month for perfect attendance. Whammo. A whole lot of people who had been consistently unable to get to work on time and had more grandmothers dying than there are idiots in Congress were suddenly able to show up every single day right on time, buffed 'n' shined and ready to work. Amazing. There were four, however, who just couldn't get with the Program. Two of them were fired shortly into my tenure. But the other two stood in the back of the room every month, frowning and shuffling their feet, as I handed out $100.00 bills to the others. Not surprisingly, one of those two could really have used the extra $100.00. Her need did not interest me in the slightest. I was very happy to leave her wage low and reward the others who excelled. (Sad commentary that showing up on time every day constituted excellence, but you've got to start somewhere.)

A friend of mine at the time owned a fairly large assembly

plant. He divided the workers into two teams, each with a captain. Each week, the team with the fewest quality control errors and best on-time completion rate was declared the winner. Its captain got $100.00; every team member got $50.00. In the late '70s, to minimum-wage assembly workers, this meant something. And every two weeks, he switched captains, so each captain got the other one's team. Every so often he shuffled up the teams. It shouldn't surprise you that, in 48 work weeks, one of the captains won 36 times—75%. It reminded me of the old quote attributed to the great college football coach Bear Bryant: "I'll beat you with my team in the first half, then we can switch, and I'll beat you with your team in the second half." Something close to that anyway. I'm not a Bear historian and I'm not going to the trouble to hunt down the precise quote. Point made. Winners win, losers lose. In this case, the best-performing supervisor made an extra $3,600.00 for the year; the, uh, runner-up made an extra $1,200.00. As it should be.

I have, over the years, personally had individual employees to whom I've paid yearly bonuses—by formula—as large as 300% of their base salaries. Happily. I've also had employees who got the cursory minimum, a $25 gift card and a "Ho, ho, ho."

CHAPTER 26

When Bonuses Become Obligations

Alimony is like buying oats for a dead horse.

—Bugs Baer, newspaper columnist

I was hanging around in a client's office one Friday, right before lunch, waiting for him. I heard his staff talking about "pizza Friday"—for hitting the office's sales quota for the week, he sprung for pizza, sub sandwiches, and soft drinks for everybody. Apparently this happened frequently. One staff person told the others: "And the cheap bastard orders from whatever place he has coupons for!"

I made this kind of mistake myself years back, when I had a lot of employees. Confusing "bonuses" with "being nice." If bonuses become routine, then they become expected, then they become a valueless expense. Maybe you remember the

Christmas movie starring Chevy Chase, in which he and his entire family are so expectant of his Christmas bonus that, when it isn't forthcoming, all manner of mayhem ensues including, as I recall, a kidnapping of the boss.

We should begin with a philosophical position. Many people view bonuses as rewards for jobs generally done well or, in my opinion, worse, a requisite sharing of the wealth from the business's prosperity. I strongly disagree with this premise. Just throwing money around without securing measurable return on investment is in violation of your chief responsibility as CEO: to maximize profits for invested shareholders. You may be CEO and sole shareholder. Doesn't alter your mandate. And, as my "cheap bastard" anecdote illustrates, you can't buy morale or compliance this way. My position is that bonuses should buy something of value that you can clearly and definitively measure. Bonuses may be used to correct unprofitable behavior, encourage profitable behavior, encourage education and self-improvement, encourage doing difficult or uncomfortable things. They are not gifts or obligations; they are tools.

NO B.S. Ruthless Management Truth #7

Bonuses should buy something of value.

Let's also clarify the difference between "bonuses" and "recognition." Getting the employee-of-the-month parking space, for example, is recognition. It is not a bonus. A bonus is money, extra time off, or things money buys, like vacations or merchandise. Recognition is pins, plaques, newsletter articles, parking spaces.

Bonuses are very troublesome things, and team or group bonuses are the most difficult. Frankly, I'm not convinced there are any good answers to this conundrum, although some seem worse than others. I've had many business owners and smart consultants all show me their "plans" for bonus compensation, and I've found them all flawed, one way or another.

I'm not a fan of group bonuses tied to sales, because far too much of that outcome is outside the control of the employees, and the reward is almost always overly generous to some and miserly to others. The best results seem to come from very targeted, behavior-based, individual bonus plans. These are usually engineered to get an employee to do something he tends to avoid, neglect, or find uncomfortable or difficult, often connected to making that employee and his job function more profitable for the company. Such bonuses do, however, become obligations. If you take away the bonus compensation, the bought-and-paid-for compliance also goes away. Such institutionalized bonuses can be perfectly OK and profitable, but you need to realize what you're getting into before you start. Undoing any is ugly.

Even on a group level, it's best to narrow the focus of the result rewarded by bonuses to what's very much in the control of the people in that employee group. Consider an office or showroom where prospects come by appointment to meet with a salesperson. The three people fielding the phone calls from prospects responding to advertising have near total control over how many such calls convert to kept appointments, but they have little if any control over how many convert to customers or how much they buy. Tying their bonuses to sales can be "demotivating," especially if the sales reps are having a slump. Or consider a service business, like a restaurant or a dry cleaner. The counter clerk, cleaning folks in the back room, chef and cooks, concierge and car valets have little or no control over total sales, as that depends a lot on the effectiveness of the business's advertising and marketing, pricing, and possibly even physical location. But they all have considerable impact on customer retention and repeat business.

How to Assemble Your Bonus Plans

In developing bonus opportunities for individual employees or groups of employees, you have to think about what "extra effort" behavior you want to try to buy, what it's worth to you, and what you are willing to pay for it.

Next, you have to figure out what will be most motivating to the person or people you are trying to buy extra effort from with your bonuses. Money may or may not be the right answer, all or part of the time. For example, in a marketing test I conducted for a client, offering $100.00 cash or a choice of a $100.00 Wal-Mart®, Olive Garden® Restaurants, or Bed, Bath & Beyond® gift card, three times as many people opted for the gift card. Why? Given cash, they would feel compelled to pay bills with it. Given a gift card, they feel free to go and splurge and buy themselves something they want. If given $750.00 cash, they might feel compelled to pay off a big credit card balance—and certainly not to run off to Atlantic City for the weekend. But being given a weekend at an Atlantic City hotel, room, meals, a show, and $100.00 cash to gamble with might be much more inspiring. You also have to decide whether to rotate different incentives and bonuses during the year, tied to the same behavior being purchased and rewarded, or to lock in the same bonus every month. You should also consider the frequency of bonuses or at least the frequency of measuring progress toward them.

Finally, you have to decide whether to institutionalize the bonus plan or to set it up as a temporary and short-term program that will go away and be replaced with a different one.

The last thing about this I'd like to say is that bonus plans shouldn't be considered out of context of your entire compensation scheme. Most employers act as if they are paying people to show up. In reality, you are attempting to purchase certain behaviors and results connected to those behaviors, cooperative and even enthusiastic compliance with your Program. So, all compensation should be tied as clearly and directly as possible to those objectives. Woody Allen was probably right when he said that one-third of success is just showing up. But in managing people, it's the other two-thirds we really have to worry about!

CHAPTER 27

Motivation by Measurement

BY BILL GLAZER

After I graduated from college, I went into the family menswear retail business. After my father retired, I took the helm and we achieved Herculean growth. I opened our second location in 1991 and the business grew to become the two most successful menswear retail stores in Maryland, employing as many as 65 wonderful people.

Then in 1998, at the urging of Dan Kennedy, I opened up a marketing company providing retailers in all categories "cutting-edge," cost-effective advertising and marketing advice to help them attract more new customers, improve customer retention, and increase customer spending.

I guess I was a pretty good student of Dan's because in 2003 he asked me to take over the day-to-day operation of his business, which is now called Glazer-Kennedy Insider's Circle™, providing marketing and moneymaking advice to more than 130,000 business owners and entrepreneurs throughout the world. During the first three and a half years of running this business with Dan, we've grown by more than 2000%.

The one thing that has never changed, whether I was operating a menswear business or running a multimillion-dollar marketing company, has been hearing owners and upper management complain about the people who work for them. They complain because their employees don't do things the way that they would do it themselves. The unfortunate reality is that complaining about your employees does absolutely nothing to fix the problem.

In fact, I'm convinced that the entire population is divided into basically two groups. Group #1 is what I call the "5 Percenters." This is the 5% of the work force that contains entrepreneurs and business owners.

Group #2 is the "95 Percenters," meaning that 95% of all people fall into this group. These are the employees who report to the 5 Percenters. Here's a very radical idea for you. We need the 95 Percenters as much as we need the 5 Percenters because without them, **nothing would ever get done.**

Think about it! Without the 95 Percenters, who would make and serve our coffee at the coffee shop every morning . . . . who would make sure our customers, clients, or patients are taken care of . . . . more importantly, who would make sure we achieve our goals?

Along my entrepreneurial journey, I met a lot of people who made a very big impact on my thinking about the science of management. Probably the person who has made the biggest impact is a management coach by the name of Vince Zirpoli. I remember when I first met Vince he told me his definition of management, which I have adopted now as my own, since I think it is the best I've ever heard.

Here is Vince's definition of management:

GETTING THINGS DONE THROUGH OTHERS.

I am not a fan of "motivation" as most people too often think of it—the weekly, occasional, or even random pep talk, the occasional seminar, theme buttons and posters. In fact, it is my belief that motivation without measurement and involvement is meaningless.

Following are two of the best methods I've relied on for getting things done through others, which feature measurement and involvement.

Method 1: Measure Everything That's Important and Post It

Think about what happened the last time you went to a professional baseball game. The first batter walked to the plate and the big electronic screen posted his name and all his relevant statistics. It gave you his batting average, how many home runs he had hit, how many games he had played, and a host of other statistical information.

Why do they do that?

For one thing, it is a way for the people in the stands to evaluate the quality of the player.

Also, it serves as a motivation for the batter. Don't you think that he wants to have really great personal statistics up there on a huge screen for thousands of people to see, including his manager, his fellow players, and the team owner? If he has pride, it's got to motivate him to try to do better.

Most entrepreneurs and people in management don't really know how well their employees are doing. For example, when I was in retail, I found that most retail store owners would track each of their salesperson's sales. That's good, but it's not enough.

The only way you are going to find out is by measuring everything that's important.

Some people think that's wrong. They don't measure much of anything. They tell people, "Just go out there and do the best job that you can."

That's wrong.

It's wrong because doing the best job that you can may not be good enough. Just like in baseball. If everyone on the team is batting between .225 and .310, a .115 player is not going to be in the lineup even if he is doing the best job he can.

That's why you need to measure everything that's important.

Think of all of the different things that, when measured, can give the result you want and exactly what is acceptable performance.

Every day at my retail stores we posted our EPR (Employee Productivity Report). We wanted to know how everyone was doing, and equally important, we wanted the salespeople to know how they were performing.

Let me tell you how we did it as an example of the thinking that went into our EPR. I'm showing you this so you can use it as a guide to help you manage your own business . . . ***regardless of whatever business you're in.***

Every month we measured 15 different categories that we had diagnosed that led to acceptable productivity. They were

1. % OF TOTAL DAY: The percentage of the total sales that every salesperson sold for each specific day.
2. $/DAY: The dollar amount that the salesperson sold each day.
3. UNITS: How many items the salesperson sold each day.
4. RECEIPTS: How many different receipts the salesperson generated each day.
5. AVERAGE SALE: The average amount of each of the salesperson's transactions.
6. UPT: The average number of units of each transaction.
7. AVG DAILY $: The average amount of each sale for each day.
8. PROJ. 4 WKS: Based on the salesperson's performance to date, what his projected sales volume would be.
9. KIT PHONE: How many "Keep-in-Touch" phone contacts the salesperson made that day with his previous customers and how many appointments he made. (NOTE: More than 30% of our sales were by appointment . . . in a menswear store!)
10. KIT WRITE: How many "Thank-You" notes the salesperson wrote that day to customers who recently purchased from her.
11. KIT APPS: How many appointments showed up for that salesperson that day.

12. KIT APPS $: How much total sales the appointments generated for that day.
13. E-MAIL: How many e-mail addresses the salesperson gathered that day.
14. REFERRALS: How many referrals the salesperson received from her clients that day.
15. CC: How many store credit card accounts the salesperson opened that day.

These are the items that we decided to measure that made sense for that company. You need to decide what categories are important for your business.

When thinking about what to measure, consider these questions:

1. Is the statistic important?
2. Is the statistic trackable?
3. Will the employee understand the statistic?
4. Does the statistic measure what you want to measure?

When we first put this program into effect, it met a lot of resistance. Salespeople told us that it wasn't right for other people to see their performance. Funny thing was that these were the same salespeople who had lower performance.

We found that in a short period of time, two very interesting things happened.

First, we experienced some turnover by the underperforming salespeople. These were the same people who should have gone. They were not the right fit for the job.

Second, the performance of the salespeople who remained rose significantly. What we discovered was that good salespeople are naturally competitive. They'll try to be the top in each category measured.

The chart that we posted that showed each of the 15 categories of statistics was updated daily and was right outside my office. Every day our sales associates walked by, stopped, and studied the chart. They liked it because they knew exactly how they were doing and where they stood.

This was so successful that we rolled out the program to our entire staff including tailors, cashiers, receiving, and clerical. So don't think this is just for people in sales. Every company who employs people can (and should) develop measurable performance criteria.

There are several things to consider when you determine what to measure. You should start out slow. I wouldn't track more than five categories the first year; you can add categories in future years. Also, I would annually re-evaluate what is being measured. Go back and ask yourself the four questions listed earlier.

Method 2: Catch People Doing Things Right

Whenever you see an employee doing something right, say, *"CAUGHT-YA!"*

A "CAUGHT-YA!" Program is one of the great ways you can show "Your Employees Are Just as Important as Your Customers," and it's a great way to encourage them to continue to perform this activity.

The Program is simple but very effective:

1. Any employee can catch any other employee doing things right.
2. The employee that witnesses someone else doing things right fills out a "CAUGHT-YA" Form (see Figure 27.1) and

puts it in the "CAUGHT-YA" box, which is located in a designated area of the business.

3. Every month, a designated manager goes through the "CAUGHT-YA" Forms and selects the best "CAUGHT-YA's."
4. The "CAUGHT-YAs" are rewritten on Super Star Award Certificates (see Figure 27.2) and posted on the employee bulletin board.
5. At the end of the month, the "CAUGHT-YA" employee is presented the Award Certificate when all of his fellow employees are present.

Now what do you think happens?

Simple . . . people love to be caught. It feeds their ego. So they start doing things right. When they're caught, they do more things right, because they love the attention they receive. It's contagious. It's the one disease that you want everyone to catch.

Now you have the two best methods that I have ever seen to get the 95 Percenters to perform up to the level you want them to. Obviously each of these methods works independently of the other, but as you can imagine, when you implement them both, they work even better.

BILL GLAZER is the Number-One Most Celebrated Marketing Consultant specializing in the Retail Industry. Retailers should visit his web site at www.bgsmarketing.com. All others should visit www.dankennedy.com to sign up for The Most Incredible FREE Gift Ever, containing well over $700.00 of pure moneymaking information for any business.

FIGURE 27.1: "CAUGHT-YA" Form

CAUGHT-YA

Nomination

Employee:

____

Action:

____

____

____

____

____

____

Caught By:

____

Date:

____

FIGURE 27.2: Super Star Certificate

CHAPTER 28

Is a Happy Workplace a Productive Workplace?

We have to pursue this subject of "fun" very seriously if we want to stay competitive in the 21st century.

—George Yeo, then Singapore's Minister of State for Finance and World Affairs

"Happy" is such a subjective idea.

I know one employee who is extremely productive and a real nose-to-the-grindstone gal, who detests all distractions. She hates birthday celebrations, radios playing in cubicles, people hanging around engaged in casual conversation. She wants everybody to leave her the hell alone so she can work. She prefers hearing 5 words to 50. This makes her happy. I visited another client's company with nearly 100 employees and found something that looked more like *Animal House* than *Work Place*. Wildly, individualistically decorated work areas, people zipping through the office on skateboards, impromptu meetings left and right, three people shooting baskets at the end of the hall while discussing solutions to a key account's unhappiness, and lunch extended that day by a half hour to watch somebody, I forget who, on *The View*. The owner insists his crew is infinitely more productive if happy and happiest if free to have fun. It ain't your daddy's Buick® factory. I suspect somewhere between the extremes lies the sweet spot for your business.

You don't want your people living the life of the doughnut shop manager in the old Dunkin' Donuts® commercial, seen slowly dragging himself from bed and sadly mumbling, "Time to make the donuts," as he shuffled off to work. You don't want "the gray man syndrome": a business populated with people gray of pallor, gray of dress, gray of mind. But I am pretty certain you don't want a perpetual Chuck E. Cheese® party going on either.

I hear of—and occasionally see—these happy 'n' fun workplaces from time to time, often glorified and celebrated in business media, and I am skeptical.

At the very beginning of my career, when I entered the advertising business, I had a picture in my mind of incredibly creative people sitting around smoking funny stuff and batting about ideas. The real development of effective advertising looks nothing like that at all. I have since discovered that no business is much like what it seems to outsiders. Most businesses' success has a whole lot more to do with organized, disciplined, machine-like work than with fun. As a professional speaker, for example, I made more than a million dollars a year for the ten years I chose to hopscotch the country working every week. I did it with a precisely crafted, scripted presentation that drove people in stampedes to buy my books and audio programs, and I delivered it with such robotlike consistency I came to understand it as very highly paid factory labor, and, frankly, it wasn't much fun. That's not to say I didn't enjoy the camaraderie of the other speakers and the audiovisual team or some of the people I met or some of the places I went; I did. But the fun was "around" the work, not in the work itself. The work was high stress, high pressure, and mind numbing. I've been an insider of sorts in more than 150 different kinds of businesses. The successful ones all have this in common: work that isn't much fun.

There's a profound difference between enjoying your work and the people you work with, doing work you're confident at, good at, and proud of, feeling rewarded by work . . . and trying to turn work into *fun*.

Fun

You might, at this point, think I'm opposed to people enjoying their jobs, let alone having fun at work. Actually, nothing could be further from the truth. In fact, the company I admire above all others, marvel endlessly at, and study constantly (and own stock in) is Disney®. Southwest Airlines®, with its happy, singing, joking flight attendants and consistently sky-high levels of customer satisfaction, also merits a spot on "The Most Interesting Companies" list.

Many business owners inspired by examples like these, who are eager to emulate them, misunderstand what they are observing.

The two companies I just named—and many others celebrated for their wildly creative workplaces and people having so much fun at work that it's play—are actually in the entertainment business. Their workplace is a stage for performers and performance. The much used example of the Pike Place Fish Market in Seattle is in this category. An entire popular "have fun at work" training and consulting company, with bestselling books, badges, hats—named Fish—was built around this singular example. Southwest Airlines® created its "goofy culture" to entertain passengers; to substitute its low level of service—early on, all it could afford—for competing airlines' reserved seating, available first class, meals, and movies. These companies' strategies do not necessarily transfer wholesale to businesses not in the entertainment industry.

On the other hand, there's nothing wrong with people enjoying their jobs and the people they work with and the environment they work in, so some aspects of the "happy place" ideal can transfer to just about any business—with caveats. So . . .

Beneath the happy, fun veneer of these companies lies a comprehensive, microdetailed, and aggressively enforced collection of policies that keep tight control over what seems to be footloose and fancy-free employees . . . and that focus on, measure, and manage profits. To the casual observer, it may seem improvisational. To the insiders, it is rigidly choreographed. And beware: most books lauding these highly "creative" companies delight in telling anecdotes that further the legends, that strengthen the idea easiest to sell—that just creating a happy place and letting happy people loose in it will somehow create profits. These books devote little or no attention to the rigid choreography.

At Disney®, for example, I took a group of my clients to a private luncheon with two Imagineers. When questioned by my smart group, they were loathe to discuss anything about the "management by numbers" that goes on in the parks, at a microscopic level. Pressed, they admitted that everything and everybody is intently measured. For example, the cheerful store clerks wearing all the little collectible pins on sashes who seem to be having just boatloads of FUN trading pins with kids are each monitored for pin sales, by location, by shift, by person, by same day prior year, and by other factors that determine whether that person continues as a pin trader or not. The clerks who do the best at selling a lot of pins this way obviously do enjoy it and have fun doing it, but their fun is managed for profit.

Disney is also an intensely hierarchal environment, with managers on top of managers on top of managers, supervisors on top of supervisors, enforcing very rigid Programs. Disney is all about tightly scripted performances, from the answering of a phone to the handling of a frustrated customer. All the FUN you see going on around you is occurring within some very tight and narrow parameters—kind of like watching a couple of dogs playing in a small yard confined by the Invisible Fence®. You can't see that fence with the naked eye. But it's there.

At Southwest, the company's profits depend on "the ten-minute turn"; its unique, never replicated ability to consistently land, empty, clean, and fill up an airplane in just ten minutes. That puts massive pressure on the crews to perform. It is a micro-choreographed process administered with zero tolerance for deviations and not even a millisecond for people to tell each other jokes. The checklist is carved in cement, the race is on, and woe be to the employee who derails this process—whether he's having FUN or not.

In short, all the "fun stuff" works only if paired with several other essential elements, none of which are "fun" to talk about or implement. If you try replicating just the fun stuff without these other essentials, you'll be a crying clown seated on a hard bench in a very unfunny place: bankruptcy court.

THE CLOCK ON THE WALL

Vincent Palko
www.AdToons.com

CHAPTER 29

Hire the Thick-Skinned

Immense power is acquired by assuring yourself in your secret reveries that you were born to control affairs.

—Andrew Carnegie

I find Donald Trump fascinating. There is a very negative, critical book about him written by an obviously bitter ex-employee. Included in its criticism is a portrayal built by anecdotes of Trump as a belligerent, bellicose, outrageously demanding, harshly critical boss from hell. I've talked with Bill Rancic, the first year's *Apprentice* winner, about working for Trump. Bill jokingly said the person who finished second and didn't get the job might have really been the winner. I'm quite sure working for Trump is no Sunday picnic.

Actually, every highly successful entrepreneur I've ever been around is a boss from hell by many of his employees' and ex-employees' definitions. To paraphrase a famous President, "Give 'em Hell" Harry Truman: bosses of high-profit companies don't give 'em hell. The employees just think it's hell.

In her book *Ballsy*, the very talented and clever author Karen Salmansohn writes: "There are no wishy-washy rock stars. No wishy-washy astronauts. No wishy-washy Nobel prize winners. No wishy-washy CEO's." As a matter of fact, everybody in the superhigh achiever category is pushy, demanding, impatient, intolerant, prone to losing their cool, screaming, throwing things, and sending the weak-minded and weak-willed scurrying for cover. Most of us simply have no time to be gentle.

Back to the book about Trump, one of the author's criticisms of Trump was about his unreasonable fetish for pristine cleanliness in his hotels. I'll tell you something I told Donald Trump personally, when we were speaking at the same event: I have stayed in thousands of hotels and put on meetings and conferences of all sizes in hundreds of hotels. I have spent fortunes in the highest-regarded hotels, including Ritz-Carltons® and Four Seasons®. When I took a small client group to the Trump Plaza® in Atlantic City for a two-day mastermind meeting, I had low expectations. I realize that Atlantic City isn't Las Vegas. My preconception of the property was as a gingerbreaded-up Motel 6® with slot machines. I even warned my group not to be grumpy about accommodations or service. To my pleasant surprise, I can say that I have never been treated as professionally, courteously, and cooperatively by every single member of a hotel's staff anywhere else. I never once heard the word *no*. Even though ours was a tiny group of little apparent economic importance to the hotel, our every request was greeted with pleasant, prompt response. The service was, for example, infinitely better than that at the much hyped Bellagio in Vegas. The facility was clean and well attended to. The food, terrific. Somebody running this joint is doing a whole lot of things right. If that's out of abject fear of hearing Trump scream "You're Fired!" well, I'm all for it.

I work mostly with entrepreneurs, not corporate executives. My advice to entrepreneurs is: Hire the thick-skinned. Hire people who can perform under pressure, will be unfazed by your outbursts and tantrums, will be responsive to sudden and urgent demands, can turn on a dime, give as good as they get, play tough. Do *not* hire the gentle or fragile of disposition to work anywhere in close proximity to you or in direct relationship with you.

If you are a highly charged, hard-driving, highly successful entrepreneur, then quite a bit of the time you aren't going to be a lot of fun to be around, especially for the thin-skinned. But you should *not* change. I've come to appreciate that the successful entrepreneur is a unique and delicately balanced combination of dysfunctions, bad habits, personality defects as well as incredible genius, daring, and drive. You don't want to tinker with that. What works for you works, and you need people around you who can adapt to the strange creature in their midst; *you* shouldn't be adapting to suit *them.*

Let's assume we have an extremely fast, rocket-fueled, high-performance racing car with more than enough speed to win every race of the year. But it's damnably hard to handle. Its raw speed and brute power make it hard to control and intimidating to drive. It is stripped of all comforts, so driving it at maximum speed strains every muscle, jostles every body organ, and, with most people, would bring up breakfast every time. It has no air-conditioning; it generates furnacelike heat. It is ultraresponsive, so even the slightest, tiniest false move with hand or foot can

NO B.S. Ruthless Management Truth #8

Be wary of fixing yourself to suit "them." Remember, they work for you!

send it into a screaming tailspin. What do we do with this machine? Do we re-engineer it so Granny can handle it without soiling her girdle? Or do we find a driver made of all the right stuff who's a match for this machine, who can win with this machine, and then support him and it with the fastest, smartest, toughest pit crew available on the planet? You, my friend, are this machine. You need to be surrounded by and supported by people who appreciate what you are, can handle your most challenging characteristics, and can work with you to obtain optimum performance.

CHAPTER 30

Managing the Sales Process

The ultimate disease of our time is vagueness of expectations.

—JOE D. BATTEN, AUTHOR OF THE CLASSIC *TOUGH-MINDED MANAGEMENT*

In most businesses, sadly, selling is an act, not a process. The mistakes made here are many. Everything is separated and isolated. Advertising. Marketing. They deliver a prospect to Sales, where, typically, the entire outcome is placed in the hands of very fallible Salespeople permitted to freelance at will, committing random acts of Selling. Afterward, the customer is dumped off to Operations, where the promises made may or may not be fulfilled.

Examine just about any business with more than one person doing the selling and you'll find each salesperson doing things differently than the others. Over in accounting, everybody's using the very same bookkeeping ledgers, and 2 + 2 = 4, period. But in sales, for some crazy rationale, everybody's allowed to "wing it." If you want maximum profits, you'll figure out what the best sales presentation is and everybody will use it. You need a Program for selling that all your salespeople comply with and use.

Wrapped around the human salespersons adhering to your Program, you need a complete system for selling, for moving each prospect neatly along a path—or, as the marketing wiz behind BluBlockers® and author of the terrific sales and marketing book *Triggers*, Joe Sugarman, calls it, a "greased chute"—that connects advertising to marketing to selling, that qualifies and prepares prospects to buy before they consume the time and talent of your salespeople, and that both supports and helps control the efforts of the salespeople. One of the best quotes about all this is from a highly respected sales trainer, David Sandler, founder of the Sandler Selling System®, now with trainers and offices nationwide. David said: "If you don't have a system for selling, you are at the mercy of the customer's system for buying." I would add: and for not buying.

Such a system has to be built at the macro and micro levels.

The macro parts link all your advertising, marketing, publicity, sales, and operations pieces together with common themes, a clearly understood covenant with customers, and, as I said, a process for moving the customer smoothly along the path, from first expression of interest to completed purchase. Think of this as an exercise in control over the prospect and the process. The micro parts have to do with all of the human interaction between the prospect and receptionists, clerks, and, most of all, salespeople. Think of it as an exercise in control over the actual selling and the people doing the selling.

There's a lot of nonsense spewed about leaving salespeople to their own devices to preserve spontaneity, encourage creativity, and so on. It's all b.s. Selling is a scientific and mechanical process, not something you should make up as you go along. The person widely judged as America's #1 Sales Trainer, Tom Hopkins, and I are both strong advocates of scripts. As a direct-response copywriter paid upwards of $50,000.00 plus royalties to write advertisements, sales letters, and web sites, I can assure you that choice of words, that is, language, matters. What I do in writing is "salesmanship in print." If it matters there, it matters in "salesmanship live," too. But "live," not only do words chosen, scripted, and used matter, so do appearance, dress, physical movement and body language, the selling environment, the actual movement of the prospect from place to place, seating choices, props used, and much more. My colleague Sydney Biddle Barrows and I call this Sales Choreography®. We believe that everything should be choreographed, from the first step the

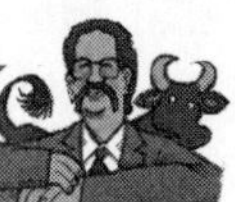

Recommended Resource #6

Information about Sydney Biddle Barrows's Sales Design® resources and tele-seminar series, her Sales Design®/Sales Choreography® consulting services, on-site sales and customer service training, and availability for speaking engagements can be obtained at www.SydneyBarrows.com.

prospect takes into the selling environment, moment by moment, movement by movement, sentence by sentence. There's quite a bit of resistance to this idea, of course, because it requires a lot of thought, discipline, and practice by the salespeople and other staff members and a lot of supervisory enforcement by management. I can assure you that, for the few who embrace it, the payoff is enormous.

Incidentally, I push my readers, newsletter subscribers, coaching members, and clients toward a "whole approach." Most of my work has to do with everything leading up to the sale. I devise the systems as well as write the copy that gets ideal prospects to raise their hands, step forward, and step onto the path constructed to then move them through qualifying and preparation, so by the time they face a salesperson or a buying decision, they view the salesperson as an expert and trusted advisor, see the company as unique, and are predisposed to do business with them. And I teach business owners how to do this for themselves. I have consultants and service providers I recommend if intense work on driving traffic online to web sites or renting mailing lists or the handling of inbound calls or software systems to manage lead flow (see next chapter) is needed. At the point that the prospect begins engaging humans, and will be face-to-face with staff and salespeople, there are resources and a telecoaching program on SalesDesign® that I've developed with Sydney Biddle Barrows, and Sydney does go on-site as well. SalesDesign® is about mapping out step-by-step-by-step everything that is to occur with and be said to the prospect, every if-he-says-this, you-say-that movement forward toward purchase. You can get much better acquainted with all of this by accepting my offer of two months' Membership in Glazer-Kennedy

Insider's Circle,™ including my *No B.S. Marketing Letter* and audio CDs—*free*—on page 350 of this book.

The Biggest Improvement You Can Make as Manager and as Sales Manager: Stop Accepting Less Than You Should Get

If you get nothing else from this book, do nothing else as a result of this book, you ought to at least take a fresh, analytical, tough-minded look at what you are getting from your people as a whole and individually for the money you are spending.

Most business owners accept shockingly poor sales results as if they make sense. In the hearing aid industry, the "close rate"—people who come to the store, get a hearing test, and get a full sales presentation—ranges from as poor as 25% to as good as 40%. Out of every 100 people, 60 to 75 who come in suffering from hearing difficulties and in need of a hearing aid do NOT buy! How can anyone managing this business accept such a thing? In the automobile business, roughly 20% of the people who come into a showroom buy a car there. That means 80 of the 100 left their homes, got in their cars, drove across town to the car dealership, braved the selling environment, looked at, asked questions about, even test-drove cars that interested them but then were not sold a car. To me, incredible. Awful. Embarrassing. Yet car sales managers confronted about this shrug and tell me, "That's about right." No. It isn't. In a dental practice, chiropractic practice, or the like, patients coming in for consultation and exam are subsequently given a sales presentation. Here I see wildly differing results. One doctor will close 70%, another a pathetic 30%. Why the difference?

In the last comparable, completely controlled selling environment I managed myself, we brought doctors into a small meeting of several hours to group sell a product. We had one employee doing these meetings in about 25 cities a month and I did them in 5 a month. In three years, his close rate was never—never—below 85%. Mine hovered at 80%. Most of the time, he closed all but one person, whom he called the next day and closed after the fact. I have been told by many others trying to replicate this model or with experience in this type of selling that such numbers are "impossible" and that he and I must be "freaks of nature." They're wrong. Not only are such results possible, but they should be expected, normal, and customary. We achieved them for reasons anyone *can* replicate in *any* business: at the macro level, we had a system delivering interested, qualified, prepared prospects to our selling environment; at the micro level, we had a precisely crafted presentation delivered perfectly.

If people come to buy, they ALL should buy. If that's not happening, you should be racking your brain to figure out what you are doing wrong.

The Human Factor: If You Are Going to Have Salespeople in Your Employ, Pick Carefully and Manage Tough

It's not just "Can they sell?" It's "Will they sell?" and "Will they sell here?" I learned this from a top sales management consultant, Bill Brooks, and it is profound. It's not just limited to salespeople, either, it really applies to every type of employee in every type of job. Reality is, somebody who might be a good employee at Company A may be a lousy employee in the same job at Company B.

This is what makes hiring by resume so flawed.

But how can this be? After all, auto sales is auto sales, so a guy who was successful at the Cadillac dealer in Chicago ought to succeed at the Cadillac dealership in Cleveland, and the guy who was successful at the Cadillac dealership in Chicago should thrive at the Lexus dealership in Chicago. And the person who was a super receptionist at one financial planner's office will surely be just as super at another financial planner's office, right? Wrong.

Different people flourish or flunk in different environments.

Let's start back at the first question: Can he sell? If you are hiring experienced salespeople, then you can answer this question by looking at their experience to date, checking their references, seeing proof of their commissions earned. If you are hiring inexperienced people and making them into salespeople, then you might rely on much more in-depth interviews including discussing what they think is the right thing to do in different selling situations. You might utilize an aptitude test purchased from one of the many companies that provide assessment tests. And you'll be looking for nonsales experience that evidences the attitudes necessary for success in selling. For example, one client of mine with a very successful sales organization, who hires only people with no prior selling experience, asks, "Have you been successful in anything?" and "Have you struggled and found something so difficult you almost quit but then stuck with it and succeeded?"

The second question: **Will he sell?** Again, if recruiting experienced salespeople, you can look into their historical track record. If they had peaks and slumps and inconsistent results where they were, you'd need a good reason to believe they aren't going to import their inconsistency into your business. If they increased their sales and earnings year to year, you could hope for that same pattern in your employ. If they stagnated, you'd need good reason to expect otherwise. Sometimes just the change of scenery will revitalize a bored or complacent experienced pro, but that will usually be brief. If he got complacent there, he'll get complacent here. When considering "Will he sell?" you're trying to solve the mystery of motivation, and that's not easy. But self-motivation leaves clues. The most recent sales book he's read, most recent sales seminar he's been to, most interesting technique he's introduced to his repertoire in the past year. What he can tell you about his goals. If hiring inexperienced people for sales, again, you have no specific history to consider, but you do have nonspecific history, basically the person's whole story. Did he work two jobs to get through school or did mommy pay his way? Has he worked in any job dealing with the public, like waiting tables? Is he really interested in a sales career or settling for it because he can't find what he wants? If he's interested, he'll already be reading books, listening to CDs, and educating and preparing himself.

The third question is the trickiest. Just because he can and will sell does not mean he'll excel at selling in your employ. Your company culture may be very different than ones he's previously experienced. You may require him to present things in a way he feels is deceptive, dishonest, or unethical, or he may feel hamstrung and neutered by the ethical restraints you impose on the way he presents things. You may have a better-defined Program you insist be complied with than his prior employers, and he may welcome the organization and discipline, or he may chafe at it. These matters need to be explored in lengthy, frank, and detailed discussions once you get serious about a candidate. There is no point in hiring a sales professional without full disclosure of your Program and how tough you are about compliance with it.

Right Sales System + Right Salespeople = Outstanding Success

Almost. The missing link has to do with lost but viable prospects. Most systems that control everything leading up to the sale give up on prospects too soon and too easily, or leave ongoing follow-up to the human salespeople. Doing that can be a huge mistake. Salespeople really adept at selling are usually incredibly inept and irresponsible at follow-up. They are called "salespeople," not follow-up people. The next chapter talks quite a bit about plugging the leaky holes of poor follow-up. Its author is a client of mine, and I also endorse his company's unique software system. It's the one we use at Glazer-Kennedy Insider's Circle™, and most of my clients use it as well. In interest of full disclosure, I am a stockholder in this company as well.

However you accomplish it, here's what's important: once someone has raised their hand and expressed interest in your products, services, solution, or information, and you put them on your path, they should be moved forward toward the sale at a prescribed yet flexible pace, with a lot of nudges by mail, e-mail, fax, drives to different web sites, teleseminars, webinars—a primary sequence but for those who fail to move at its pace, a continuing, patient sequence. Most businesses waste the lion's share of all the money spent on advertising by, first, not using it to create and capture interested prospects and then by poor or insufficient follow-up.

Beyond that, follow-up after the sale shouldn't be left in the hands of salespeople either. They will instinctively focus on their next hunt and kill, the next prospect, the next sale. But, hopefully, you are interested in creating, measuring, and maximizing long-term customer value. To do that, you have to wow 'em after the sale and continually, frequently "arrive" to keep the relationship alive.

So, finally, you have to *manage the relationships* with your prospects and your customers.

CHAPTER 31

Maximizing the Value of Your Sales and Marketing Personnel

BY CLATE MASK

I want to talk to you candidly, from one entrepreneur to another. You have a great product or service. You have big dreams and aspirations for your business—it doesn't feel like a small business to you. You're going to make something of it. You're passionate about what you're doing. You are confident, you're working hard, and you're enjoying some success.

But you sure wish there were more of YOU to go around.

You've probably learned that effective management of your people and resources has everything to do with your bottom line. And nowhere does that ring more true than in the sales and marketing functions of your business. If you could only get more out of your sales and marketing efforts, you know your profits would soar.

If this strikes a chord with you, then this chapter will be one of the most important and exciting messages you will ever read. Because this chapter is all about the ONE thing that is sure to dramatically improve your sales.

It's all about follow-up. Follow-up, follow-up, follow-up, follow-up.

Let me start from the beginning . . .

Many years ago, my software company was providing customized software to small businesses wanting to use the power of automation to grow their companies. We built all sorts of custom software applications. Most of them had a customer management component to them.

Then one day, a guy came to us and asked us to help him more effectively manage his leads and customers. He was trying to follow up with his prospects and customers, but he was making lots of mistakes. He was having a heck of a time keeping leads, prospects, and customers organized. He couldn't track things properly and the follow-up was hit-or-miss.

So he hired us to write a software program that would help him *automatically* follow up with prospects and customers, track the communications, organize prospects and customers into groups, and run the whole follow-up function of his business. He was thrilled with what we created for him and he went away very happy.

But then he came back. Turns out, he had a bunch of mortgage broker clients who realized what his software was doing for *his* business . . . and they wanted it for *their* businesses. So, we "productized" the software program and provided it to a few dozen mortgage brokers, who began to rave about the product.

Things were going so well with our mortgage broker clients that we moved away from the custom software business and began selling our "follow-up machine" exclusively to mortgage brokers. I was doing the selling, talking to prospects, following up with leads, educating people on the benefits of our software, and so on.

And then something amazing happened.

We began to use the follow-up features of the software in our own sales and marketing efforts. Suddenly, prospects I had never talked to were calling me up, saying they were ready to buy. I was having conversations with people who had heard from me several months earlier and had been receiving my follow-ups.

Streams of prospects were coming out of the wood work, calling me, e-mailing me. They were hot and ready to buy.

That's when I knew we were on to something.

And our business has never been the same since. Today tens of thousands of people use our software every day to follow up, educate their prospects and customers, cultivate lasting relationships, and maximize the value of their prospect and customer lists. The software does many things for small businesses that want to grow fast, but "autopilot follow-up" is at the heart of it all.

What does this all mean for you? How does it apply to your management of the sales and marketing personnel in your business? Well, you don't need an army of telemarketers to do this. You DO need to know the proven secrets to mastering follow-up.

And I promise you that when you put them in play, it will change the way you do business. It will supercharge your marketing and sales in ways you never believed possible. And it will enable you to get much more productivity out of your all-critical sales and marketing personnel.

It will put your marketing on autopilot, which is the best way to get the most out of your prospect and customer lists without hiring an army of telemarketers to do your follow-up for you.

OK, so now that you know where I'm coming from, let me ask you a potentially painful question:

Are you consistently, religiously, and effectively following up with ALL of your prospects and customers?

I have asked this question to literally tens of thousands of entrepreneurs, marketers, and successful small businesses. And you know what?

Nine hundred ninety-nine times out of a 1,000, the answer is a big, fat, painful NO!

My guess is that you're no exception to the rule. No matter how well your business is doing right now, so-so, good, or GREAT, you *know* you're leaving a *ton* of money on the table.

Now let me ask you a less painful question:

What would happen to your business if you consistently, religiously, and effectively followed up with all of your prospects and customers?

Now that I think about it, maybe that question is sort of painful.

I mean, just imagine for a second how much more cold, hard cash you could have stuffed into *your* personal bank account last year if you had managed to consistently, religiously, and effectively follow up with your prospects and customers.

Five Foolproof Secrets to Follow-Up Mastery!

Here's the promise: if you'll apply these secrets to YOUR marketing, you'll get two to four times the number of sales or customers from the exact same batch of leads you'd normally be spending the long hours of night worrying yourself into an ulcer about.

An outrageous claim, I know . . . but let me be even more outrageous. Not only will you close a lot more sales from your leads, but you'll do it in less time, your margins will be higher, and your job satisfaction will be greater than ever because you'll be selling your product or service from a position of respected authority!

Secret 1: "Cherry-Picking" and the Three Types of Leads

Every time you run a marketing campaign, the leads you get can be divided into three categories:

1. leads that are ready NOW (hot);
2. leads that are not ready now but will be ready soon (warm—these leads are CRITICAL to your success); and
3. leads that may never be ready (cold or bad leads).

The problem is, you can't divide the leads into categories because you don't know which leads go into which categories.

So you or your staff members or salespeople call every lead once or twice and then you spend the time with the leads that look like they're going to close.

Every smart salesperson who works on commission does this—they go for the low-hanging fruit!

That's right. They basically cherry-pick! Cherry-picking is the natural result here because

1. sales reps are paid high commissions for a sale;
2. sales reps can't tell the difference between warm leads and bad leads until they reach them;
3. if your sales rep does reach the prospect and the timing isn't right, the sales rep doesn't have the time or patience to constantly follow up.

There's nothing wrong with your salespeople spending their time with hot leads. The problem of cherry-picking comes when they neglect all those warm leads!

Of course, everyone *says* they're going to follow up with the other leads *"one of these days,"* but the fact is, they don't do it.

Or, if they do follow up, they don't do it consistently, religiously, and effectively because, quite frankly, it's a royal pain in the neck.

Instead of doing the tedious follow-up grunt work, sales reps usually wait for a new batch of leads to come in. In the meantime, the warm leads from the last batch get cold and they are soon forgotten. Simply put, they slip through the cracks.

It's important to remember that, with your advertising and marketing expenditures, you did not just buy hot, ready-to-buy, easy-to-convert leads! You paid plenty for the warm leads and even for the cold leads, some of which will warm up over time.

Your follow-up doesn't have to be hit-or-miss, but it will be if you leave it up to your salespeople. You can get more out of your leads than you're getting right now. You need to get more out of your leads. And when you do, your profitability will soar.

Secret 2: Timing Is Everything!

Here is a very important truth: People buy when *they* are ready to buy, *not* when *you* are ready to sell.

And this means, by definition, **you have to be in front of folks when they're ready to buy.**

In other words, you have to follow up with them . . . religiously!

But truly effective follow-up is a gut-wrenching, time-consuming, tedious, and labor-intensive task that is almost impossible for the human mind to keep straight—so sales professionals simply won't do it. So:

1. You need to follow up with warm and even cold-that-may-warm prospects consistently and frequently for an extended period of time.
2. You cannot afford to leave this in the hands of your salespeople.
3. You need a system for follow-up and tools to implement the system.

Secret 3: Integrate Sales and Marketing

In most companies, the marketing department's job is to get the leads, and the sales department's job is to call on the leads and close the sale. But in between "getting the lead" and "closing the sale," there's a huge gap. If you close the gap, your profits will *skyrocket*.

To close the gap, you need to recognize that

1. marketing's job doesn't begin and end when the lead is acquired;
2. the sales job doesn't begin and end with a "heat check" phone call to each lead; *and* most important,
3. *someone* (either marketing or sales) has to be in charge of "warming the leads" that aren't hot right now but will be hot down the road.

Otherwise, your marketing department is flushing money down the toilet on leads that aren't hot right now. Literally tearing up $100.00 bills and flushing them away.

Then, your sales department is wasting time *and* money trying to close sales with prospects who aren't ready.

To sum up this problem of the gap between marketing and sales, think of it this way: every business has a lead generation department (marketing) and a lead closing department (sales), but most lack a *lead warming* department. To bridge the gap between marketing and sales, you need a lead warming department. Simple as that.

So, now that you understand the task at hand, let me give you five tips on how you can make the shift:

1. Send relevant, valuable information to every prospect regularly, relentlessly, and frequently. You need to be doing this until they buy, die, or beg you for mercy!
2. Communicate with prospects efficiently, aside from the normal, time-consuming, one-on-one methods.
3. Log all communications between your office and each prospect in an organized fashion.
4. Arm yourself and your sales reps with an arsenal of specific information you can send to prospects on request.

5. Track the progress of each lead through the sales pipeline, so you always know where every lead stands.

Secret 4: You Must Have a Living, Breathing Customer Database

If you're like most small-business owners, you want to build a business that doesn't rely heavily on outside marketing efforts. You want to maximize referrals and repeat business so that you don't have to spend your time chasing down leads and convincing folks that they should do business with you.

I talk to entrepreneurs every day who dream of having a mature customer base that provides them with lots of repeat business.

But when I ask them what they're doing to make that dream a reality, too often they answer with something like: *"Well, Clate, the longer I'm in business, the more customers I work with and the more I'll get repeat business and referrals."*

There's a lot of profit to be had by being more proactive.

This stance also assumes that your longevity in business translates to top-of-consciousness positioning with your past customers and prospects. It doesn't.

As months go by, your past customers and prospects just aren't thinking about you anymore! That's the cold, hard truth. And no matter how great your product or service is, your customers are busy living their lives. Chances are, they won't remember you. And they definitely won't mention your name at the next family picnic when Uncle Jack starts talking about the pains your product or service fixes.

If you want the strongest possible customer base, you must actively, systematically, and methodically *build your customer base.*

Your "living, breathing customer base" is much more than the prospect and customer records in your spreadsheets or file cabinet. It must be organized in a way that enables you to execute effective follow-up.

You need to actively build your customer database—every day, every week, every month! All of your contact, prospect, and customer data, order and billing information—everything—needs to be entered and stored in the database.

You need these people organized into meaningful groups. And you need the flexibility to sort through the database so that at a moment's notice you can pull up prospects or customers who might bring you more business.

For example, you might want to pull up a list of all customers who purchased product *x* within the last 12 months but did not purchase product *y*. Or, you may want to look at all prospects you worked with over the last 6 months who didn't do business with you because of a specific reason.

When you combine a solid customer database with the power of consistent, religious, effective follow-up, you are finally able to optimize the value of each and every customer.

Secret 5: Education, Repetition, and Variety

I've repeated the phrase "consistent, religious, and effective follow-up" over and over. This Secret is about what that means. But first, let's talk about what NOT to do.

Most small businesses market their products and services like this:

Step 1. Buy a bunch of leads or generate leads with a mailer or other campaign.

Step 2. Distribute leads to sales reps.

Step 3. The sales reps call on the leads to find the "hot" ones, who are ready now.

Step 4. Sales reps work with hot leads to close a quick deal.

Step 5. Sales reps throw away, postpone, or neglect the leads that aren't "hot."

Step 6. Repeat the process.

Instead, your follow-up must take a combined approach that incorporates these three elements:

1. *Education.* Your follow-up materials must inform your prospects and customers. You need to provide valuable information. If you're showing up with no value, you'll wear out your welcome fast. You need to communicate that you are on *their* side and deserve to be trusted. You'll accomplish this if you provide them with accurate, insightful information. Fact is, the sales process is confusing and intimidating for your customers. They *want* to trust you. Give them the information they need and you'll earn their trust. Help them. Serve them. Provide information and they'll appreciate you for it.
2. *Repetition.* It's a proven fact that human beings have to hear the same thing over and over before it sinks in. Marketing and sales are no different. You know your products and services like the back of your hand, but your customers don't "get it" the first time they hear the message. Don't make the mistake of thinking that if a prospect heard the pitch once, he understood it. Chances are, he didn't. Tell him again and again and again.
3. *Variety.* This doesn't mean you vary your message! You need to consistently tell your message, but your follow-up *delivery* needs variety. To maximize your sales, **you must**

use multistep follow-up sequences that incorporate and orchestrate direct mail, phone, e-mail, fax, voice, and other media! Some prospects will respond to your call, others to your e-mail or letters, and others to more innovative options, such as invitations to teleseminars or webinars.

The Five Secrets Combined Have the Strength of 500

If you combine all five of the not-so-secret secrets in this chapter into one cohesive, automated, fail-safe system, you won't just see incremental sales improvements—you'll see revolutionary transformation.

CLATE MASK, CEO of Infusion Software, actively works with businesses of all types and sizes to support their sales systems. Infusion CRM (Customer Relationship Management) was built specifically to handle multistep, multimedia follow-up campaigns easily and effortlessly for a small business or a sales team of thousands. Visit www.RenegadeMillionaireSoftware.com for information.

CHAPTER 32

Managing Sales Professionals Past Their Mental Hurdles

BY MICHAEL MIGET

In sales, there is a mysterious force that sabotages even the best-planned marketing techniques and sales presentations. This force impacts the sales staff, manager, and even the business owner. You can't see it or touch it, but you can readily observe its effects once you've been trained to spot it.

Left uncorrected, this problem will keep businesses' sales well below potential and limit growth. I've struggled with it myself in the early years of my sales career, observed it in my own sales staff, and teach the business owners in my coaching program to identify and overcome it.

Here's the problem:

Salespeople have mental hurdles—self-limiting beliefs about what they can achieve. Mental hurdles can be based on past performance or the performance that is expected from them in their current work environment. For example, when I first started in the mortgage business as a loan officer, I was expected to produce $20,000.00 each month in commissions. I averaged $2,100.00 for each loan, so I knew I had to close ten loans each month to reach my goal. That's what I did.

As time went on and I gained more expertise in selling, I was able to increase my average fee to $3,500.00 per loan. I thought, "*Hey, this is great! Now I only have to sell SIX loans each month to hit my number.*" That's exactly what my production slipped to.

Instead of thinking about how much *more* money I could have earned by keeping my production at its current level, I was focused on how I could do *less* and still make the same amount of income. My current level of income had become a mental hurdle. My mind would not think past that level of income because I had grown accustomed to it.

Years later, when I hired two new loan officers for my company, I really noticed the impact of this mental hurdle. Jim came to my company from an environment where he averaged two sales each month. On the other hand, Mark came from an environment where he averaged ten sales each month. Can you imagine what happened?

That's right; Jim continued to average two loans per month while Mark continued to close ten. They both had mental hurdles affecting their performance in my company. Their beliefs were limiting their production even though they were both good marketers using the same materials and product with the same type of customer.

The Fallacy of "The Carrot Principle"

Business owners sometimes decide that increasing commissions is a good way to get their sales staff to increase production. It seems logical to expect that if staff will receive a bigger reward for each sale, they will be more motivated to increase their sales production. Owners think, "If I just make the carrot a little sweeter, my staff will work harder to get that reward and naturally close more sales."

In my experience, this is a recipe for financial disaster. A mental hurdle of each salesperson actually tends to decrease production when commissions are raised. Typically, salespeople have a set amount of money they expect to earn each month. They produce enough sales to make that income target and then, often subconsciously, slack off because they've hit the target they are accustomed to.

Improvement to marketing processes can generate the same result. When a company replaces a "cold-calling" or traditional prospecting system with good marketing techniques, the owner anticipates the increased efficiencies will produce an increase in sales production. Since the new marketing system is designed to give sales staff more time, more qualified leads, and an improved system to increase sales and commissions, there should be a corresponding increase in production.

Imagine the owner's disappointment when the production numbers stay flat after all that effort and expense. If the owner doesn't know about this mental hurdle, he may mistakenly blame the marketing system when it's his sales staff that needs reprogramming.

Mental hurdles affect all levels of sales organizations. In my coaching with mortgage brokers, I frequently hear loan officers dream of self-employment. They are lured to work independently because they want to make more money, but they enter the deal thinking in terms of what they must do *at a minimum* to maintain their current income. This thinking limits their ability to achieve the stated goal of making more money.

Business owners limit their growth by their own unique mental hurdles as well. Owners unknowingly set goals that are based on past production, income, and methods. They have a mental hurdle about how big their business can really become. This keeps the owners from seeing and embracing opportunities for potential growth or an innovative new process.

As you can see, mental hurdles limit business growth on many levels. They keep sales staff at the same level of production, frustrate sales managers who try to improve the marketing, compensation, and environment with little or no results, and stymie owners from taking the leap into the next level of business growth.

How Much Money Are You Losing Every Month to Your Mental Hurdles?

Mental hurdles, self-limiting beliefs, are costing you money in lost sales, decreased production, and missed opportunities. These hurdles also cause frustration, stress, and disappointment. You blame your staff or yourself when sales or marketing initiatives fail when the real culprit is the belief systems of the people involved.

Ready for some good news?

Mental hurdles can be eliminated. It is possible to raise the bar on expectations so that sales staff increase production. You must change the environment, to change the thinking, to get the results you desire.

In my experience, the most effective tool for overcoming mental hurdles is the mastermind concept applied in a strategic way.

In his classic book *Think and Grow Rich,* Napoleon Hill states, "Economic advantages may be created by any person who surrounds himself with the advice, counsel, and personal cooperation of a group." Hill then describes the practices of successful men like Andrew Carnegie, Henry Ford, Harvey Firestone, and Thomas Edison, who all surrounded themselves with a mastermind group of people who provided information, personal support, and encouragement.

The power of working with a mastermind group is well documented. However, it is such a classic technique that it may be taken for granted. You've probably heard of mastermind groups, but have you or anyone you know actually participated in one?

Business owners rarely share information, especially with others in the same field. You are concerned about confidentiality of your business practices and inside information. Also, you may be reluctant to bring your weaknesses and challenges to light in a public forum. No one wants to be humiliated or admit to a problem. That's why at networking meetings when asked how your business is doing, you may lie and say, "*Great!*" even if you are worried about meeting your monthly expenses.

When I first started my business, I had the same concerns. However, when I joined a mastermind group, my business began to expand. The only way that I could overcome my mental hurdles and limiting beliefs was to surround myself with a group of successful people. When I joined a mastermind group, I was able to observe other successful business owners who had higher expectations of themselves and their businesses. They demonstrated what could be possible for my business if I could raise the bar on my own thinking and expectations. To play better golf, play with better golfers!

The openness of mastermind groups and the sharing of successful and unsuccessful business practices create an environment where mental hurdles can be overcome. I've seen my coaching group members use the power of masterminding to realize what can be possible in their mortgage businesses, share strategies, and encourage each other to greater success. This concept is so valuable that I provide a mastermind group for each person who participates in my coaching programs.

If you own a business or manage a sales team, identifying and overcoming mental hurdles should be a top priority. Join a mastermind group; expand your personal and business expectations. Learn to identify your mental hurdles and overcome them. Then, bring the concept of a mastermind to your sales staff. Share your successes in overcoming your mental hurdles. Teach your sales staff to identify their own mental hurdles and overcome them.

You don't have to become a cheerleader. However, by alerting your sales staff to the limitations of mental hurdles brought about by past experience and self-limiting beliefs, you can show them how to increase their production and their income. Establishing regular mastermind groups in your office will help you raise the expectations of each one of your employees.

MICHAEL MIGET is the owner and president of Shelter Solutions, a residential mortgage broker in St. Louis, Missouri, that specializes solely in helping homeowners achieve debt freedom. He also owns a coaching and consulting business for mortgage brokers, teaching them to implement marketing and business strategies in their own local markets. You can reach Mike via fax at (314) 291-4850 or visit his web site: www.MaverickMortgageBroker.com.

CHAPTER 33

The Top Secret Mission

We have met the enemy
and they is us.

—WALT KELLY'S POGO

Please don't mistake this book as a giant exercise in blaming the employees.

A lot of employees won't perform and need to be replaced. But a lot of employees who would perform don't, largely because nobody has ever defined what they're supposed to be doing, taken the time to explain why, and provided enough initial and ongoing training so they're able to perform if willing. Business owners who spend fortunes on advertising, fortunes building and decorating their facilities, fortunes on equipment balk at spending any money on training and are too busy to bother with it themselves. It's an epidemic: top secret missions understood only by management.

In his book *The 8th Habit*, Stephen Covey describes a poll taken of 23,000 employees drawn from a mix of companies and industries. Only 37% of these employees said they had a clear understanding of what their organization was trying to achieve. Only 20% could enunciate the direct relationship between their tasks and the business's goals. And, understandably, only 20% were "enthusiastic" about their company's goals. Covey equated it to a soccer team—that only 4 of the 11 players on the field would know which goal was theirs. Only 2 of 11 would care. Only 2 of 11 would know what position they played and what they were supposed to do.

I had a client with a relatively large company run this exercise: He wrote out, from his mind, not from a manual, job descriptions for each of his people and ranked in importance what he believed they were doing. He had them do the same. We compared the notes. No matches. Zero. Not even close. For example, for his clerks at the cash registers, he had getting customers to sign up for the e-mail newsletter as Job #1. Of five such employees in his flagship store used for this test, only two had it on their list at all!

That particular glitch was easily fixed with quick, specific training, establishing expectations, and incentives, rewarding effective performance, and summarily firing the one nonperformer. Within two weeks, the e-mail capture count went from an average of 3 per day to 30 a day, 18 to 180 a week, 936 to 9,360 a year. We had already determined that the customers receiving his biweekly e-mails were worth $20.00 more per year than customers not getting the e-mails, so this was worth $187,200.00 in the one store. He has eight stores. That's $1,497,600.00.

The loss of that dough, entirely, 100% his fault. Not the employees' fault. His. Of course he protested that. After all, he *had* told them he wanted them to ask for and collect those e-mails. As if that discharged his responsibility. What he hadn't done was make sure they understood what he expected, explained that he viewed it as their most important responsibility, trained them in the script for asking for the information, paid attention to it, tracked performance by person by day and made the comparative performance known to all, policed to be sure it was being done 100% of the time via mystery shopping and surveillance at the counters, incentivized and specifically rewarded successful performance, and quickly fired and replaced nonperformers. *His* fault. *His* fault. *His* fault.

He came to me, by the way, to have me write more effective direct-mail campaigns and ads to bring a lot more new customers through his doors. My fees for the projects he wanted would have topped $150,000.00. Increased advertising and direct-mail budgets by about $200,000.00. And still not returned $1.4 million in additional revenues. But investing a little time in training and enforcement, and paying a $1.00 bonus for each valid e-mail captured—$74,880.00 for the year—could.

This is but one little micro-example of the losses and opportunities that reside in just about every business with their root cause in the existence of top secret missions.

CHAPTER 34

Ruthless Management of Word of Mouth

Not only are the hitching posts repainted every night, the starting time is based on the temperature and humidity, so the paint will be dry when the park opens the next day.

—A DISNEY EXECUTIVE EXPLAINING AN EXAMPLE OF DISNEY'S FANATICAL ATTENTION TO DETAIL, FROM *INSIDE THE MAGIC KINGDOM*, BY TOM CONNELLAN

What your customers and your prospects tell others about their experiences with your business is infinitely more powerful than anything you can say, especially through traditional, paid advertising. You can drive the sales of goods, including bad goods supported by lousy service, with advertising in the short term. But there's not enough money and ad media and cleverness in the world to sustain a business against the forces of negative, critical customer buzz.

I was told this story by a Disney Imagineer:

Suppose we leave a piece of gum on the sidewalk there, in the hot Florida sun, and you step on it. It gets all

> up in the rubber tread of your walking shoe. Tonight in your hotel, you have to pick it out of there with a ballpoint pen. It ruins your day. At home, instead of telling eight people about the great time you had at Disney, you tell them about your miserable battle with the filthy chewing gum. That's eight people who might have gone home after hearing about your great vacation, logged on to our web site, let us send them a free DVD, and ultimately booked a vacation. Each one worth maybe $2,000.00, $3,000.00, or $4,000.00. And each of them could bring us eight more but now won't. And each of them eight. That's 512 guest families at, say, $3,000.00 each, totaling $1,536,000.00. Even more, though, since each one represents the start of another endless chain of referred guests. So, that piece of gum left there a moment too long costs us more than a million dollars.

Sure, I know what you're thinking. You're thinking that the example's ridiculous and doesn't apply to your business because everybody doesn't refer eight people or your customer value isn't $3,000.00. Or you're thinking: "Well, that's Disney, and I'm not Disney. I can't afford to have a maintenance worker in a crisp, clean, starched uniform every six feet leaping on every dropped piece of litter." And that is why Disney is Disney and you are not.

Think small, stay small; think cheap, be forever doomed to *needing* to be cheap.

That's not to say you need Disney's extreme cleanliness as one of your business's standards. I don't know whether that's true in your case or not. Elsewhere I discuss the fact that different standards are best for different businesses, and that one-size-fits-all excellence aspirations do more harm than good. It is to say that when you figure out what parts of your customers' and prospects' experiences with your business matter most to them and are most likely to lead to negative word of mouth if messed up, you need to ruthlessly manage to make certain these specific things aren't messed up.

When I bought a heavily advertised whiz-bang, high-tech bed, I had the single worst customer service experience of my life. The salesman, the delivery dispatcher, other employees, all liars. I can't recall ever being as enraged as a consumer. Ultimately, I had a vice president of the company on the phone. He and I have much in common, both direct-marketing professionals. I knew the owner of the company he'd been with previously. He knew a client of mine located in his city. Even that did no good. He insufficiently apologized, offered no remedy, and finally resorted to saying, "Well, you have to agree it's a great bed, don't you?" I thought it futile to provide a lengthy training seminar on the realities of word-of-mouth marketing. Fact is, it could be the greatest bed ever invented and ever owned by me, delivering the most restful sleep I've ever experienced and liberating me from back pain, and I would still tell everybody in my wake not to buy the damned thing. Which I've done. I killed four sales immediately, within my circle of acquaintances. And now I'm telling you and 100,000 other readers my cautionary tale about this company. Because the bed is *expected to be* the greatest bed I ever owned. They promised *that*. So if it is, that meets *minimum* performance requirements. Of far greater importance to me—and, I'll wager, many affluent consumers—is not having my valuable time abused, not being put through an agonizing and difficult process to resolve problems, not dealing with rude, uncooperative, and incompetent people, and not being lied to. This company has no significant product problems. Even though mine had two major defects, that's not what turned me into a raving critic. The company has severe management problems.

The most powerful force for good or evil in business is word of mouth. *Everybody* says so. But who really does anything to manage it? You should hear one of my Platinum coaching-group Members, Dr. Tom Orent, tell his dentist clients about the "million-dollar bathroom" he had in his dental office. Five kinds of little scented soaps and five kinds of scented hand lotions in a little basket. Another basket of sample-sized lipsticks and perfumes, for patients to take as many as they liked home. Fresh, neatly folded, high-quality hand towels that had to be laundered every night, not paper towels. And the dentists say: "Five kinds of soap? How much does all that cost? Well, I'm not going to waste money on five kinds of soap. And who has time to wash, dry, and fold towels every day?" And that's why Dr. Tom has million-dollar practices and they don't.

Word of mouth is tricky. First, it has more to do with the five soaps and towels and little cosmetic gifts than with the excellence of the core service, the dentistry. The patients expect excellent dentistry. They tell people about the unexpected. Second, your people and their interaction with your customers have far greater impact than your core products or services.

Third, negative word of mouth is much easier to get and it spreads faster and in bigger numbers than positive. Spurring a lot of positive word of mouth requires creative thought and deliberate effort. Spurring monstrous amounts of negative word of mouth requires zero creativity, zero planning, and zero effort. Just let customers go away frustrated and angry.

So, you must ruthlessly refuse to tolerate—even for a minute—anything or anyone contributing to negative word of mouth. No equivalent of sticky gum can be permitted.

The other day, I stopped at a chain sandwich shop to pick up a couple of salads to go. Waiting, I wandered over to a little display promoting the company's catering service. The large, fancy box the staff packs sandwiches in for delivery had a layer of dust on its top. Were I the manager when I found it, I would call every employee to it, scream, throw it on the floor and stomp on it, threaten the very life of anyone leaving dust in this restaurant. I would begin a daily white-glove inspection. I would make it abundantly clear that discovery of dust would be closely followed by beheadings. I would not tolerate it, sanction it, make excuses for it. That's an overreaction if you think of it as just a little dust missed that week. It's not nearly enough of a reaction if you view it as a million-dollar mistake. Further, let a little dust or gum on the floor or goopy scum on a bathroom sink slide, and you establish a direction. A policy of tolerance.

> Again, you must ruthlessly refuse to tolerate—even for a minute—anything or anyone contributing to negative word of mouth.

Conversely, you should creatively strive to stimulate positive word of mouth, by delivering not only exceptional-quality goods and services, but beyond that, unexpected extras and experiences that people are inspired to tell others about.

"ARE YOU TELLING ME, FINGERSTEIN, THAT THERE'S A DIFFERENCE BETWEEN ACTIVITY AND ACCOMPLISHMENT? DAMMIT, WHY WASN'T I INFORMED OF THIS SOONER?"
CEO

Vincent Palko
www.AdToons.com

CHAPTER 35

Activity Masquerading as Accomplishment

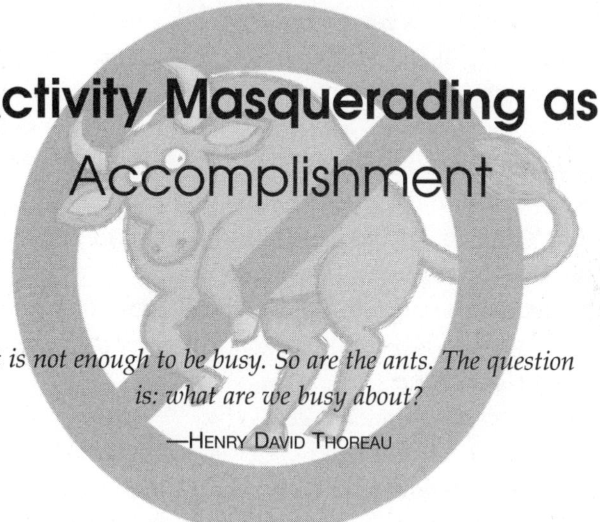

It is not enough to be busy. So are the ants. The question is: what are we busy about?

—HENRY DAVID THOREAU

If you could do nothing else but cut "activity masquerading as accomplishment" by half, you'd skyrocket any company's profits.

Some people intentionally hide their lack of accomplishment behind the mask of activity—even frantic activity. Others just can't tell the difference between the two.

So, let's begin with definitions. Defining *activity* is easy. You see it all around you and you engage in it, pretty much every minute of every day. There can be a lot of people putting in 40 hours a week and even running around while doing it with nothing getting done. Meetings held. Paper moved. Warner Brothers®

Tasmanian Devils stirring up their own little tornadoes—but when the dust settles, there's nothing to show for it.

Defining *accomplishment* is a bit more difficult, because it needs something to be measured against. It requires context.

In something like a football game, it's easy to discern the difference. A team can have a lot of activity between the 20-yard lines and never score. It can even win the game statistically, in rushing yards, passing yards, first downs, and time of possession, but still manage to lose the game on the scoreboard. Accomplishment is getting the ball into the end zone. And putting more points on the board within 60 minutes of play than the opposing team. The question of accomplishment has one answer evident to everybody in the game and everybody watching the game. It's a clear picture.

In business, it's a lot cloudier. Why?

First of all because, usually, victory or defeat can't be measured within 60 minutes. This, however, can be fixed, and the intensity and accuracy of the football game's 60 minutes can be approximated and simulated in business. Doing so is a breakthrough in personal productivity, individual productivity, and team productivity. We'll come back to that. For now, just make a mental note: a major management mistake is measuring accomplishment in too big measurements over too long a span of time. Annual or bi-annual performance reviews and quarterly earnings reports stretch the game clock out way too long and make it ridiculously easy for confusion, deliberate or accidental, of activity and accomplishment.

There's a famous story about industrialist Andrew Carnegie's right-hand man, Charlie Schwab. Charlie came up with a simple invention to increase productivity in the steel

MISSION ACCOMPLISHED

Vincent Palko
www.AdToons.com

mill—a piece of chalk. After the day shift ended, and before the night shift got to the mill, Charlie wrote a big number on the floor with chalk, the numerical measurement of the amount of steel produced during the day shift. The night shift workers didn't need it explained. They understood what it was—a challenge. And when they finished, one of them erased the old number and wrote their superior number on the floor in its place. The competition continued, night and day after day and night. I doubt something as simple would motivate many of today's factory employees. It requires competitive spirit, pride, and work ethic. But its brilliance in its time consisted of quick, simple, clear measurement. A 60-minute game. An 8-hour shift.

Second, it's cloudy and confused because of the aforementioned absence of nitty-gritty standards set up to accurately, ruthlessly judge accomplishment. If you don't know what a deer looks like, deer hunting is a waste of time and quite possibly dangerous. If you don't know what accomplishment is supposed to look like—today—how will you know whether it's sipping from the puddle in your backyard or not?

Let me make this personal. I tend to get a whole lot more accomplished every day than most people do in a week or a month. There are many ways for me to know this and I'm not going to bore you with all of them—for the sake of efficiency here, in getting to what could be useful to you, I'll ask you to take my word for it. One subjective way I know, though, is that everybody who gets to know me much, in person, or just by observing my prolific work performance and output by reading my newsletters, wants to know how the devil I do it. So many wanted to know, I wrote an entire book about it: *No B.S. Time Management for Entrepreneurs.* But here's one of the main secrets,

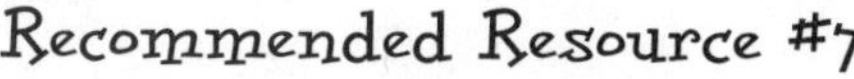

Complete information about the other books in the NO B.S. series, free sample chapters and video interviews with Dan Kennedy by Kristi Frank from Donald Trump's *The Apprentice* are available at www.NoBSBooks.com. Books are available at bookstores and online booksellers. See pages 342–344 for more information.

and it's a simple one. I decide what I am going to GET DONE . . . not start, not work on, not try to get done . . . GET DONE each day, then assign each item a block of time from five or ten minutes to a couple hours for its completion. I assign time slots and script my day in advance to the minute, then I bar all interruptions and distractions and do those things within the time allotted.

If you are willing to so organize, hold yourself ruthlessly accountable, and refuse interference, then you can get just as much accomplished as I do. Then if you want to move others up to higher levels of accomplishment, you can teach them this modus operandi and insist they use it—evidenced by sharing their day's scripts with you, at the starting gate and at the finish line.

If you are unwilling to do these four things—and unwilling to insist your key people do these four things—nothing else will save you; you are forever doomed and destined to the monstrous frustration that comes from unending, frantic activity but little accomplishment.

1. Decide what you are going to Get Done.
2. Assign each item a block of time for its completion.
3. Script your entire day minute by minute in advance, incorporating the Get Done items and their assigned blocks of time.
4. Bar all interruptions and distractions until you are Done.

One study of a large Fortune 1000 corporation's top 25 executives found that, by their own accounts, they average fewer than 40 minutes a day of actual accomplishment. Most put in 10 hours a day. Nine hours and 15 minutes a day, by their own account, could not evidence any accomplishment. It is, as they described it, time that gets away (as if a prison break); time sucked up by others; time lost forever with nothing in exchange. I don't doubt their assessments. I suspect most business owners operate with similarly depressing ratios. Yet, there's also reason for hope there. If you are getting only 40 minutes of accomplishment time out of a day, you need only get to 1 hour and 20 minutes—about the same amount of time as given to a lunch break—to triple your personal productivity. If you're at 40, it's a safe bet most of the key people working for you are at 20. This means there's a whole lot of room for more accomplishment!

So, still, exactly what *is* Accomplishment?

Something that must be done, done. Something done that either immediately produces profits or can be measured and tracked as directly contributing to sustaining or increasing profits. A problem interfering with maximum productivity or maximum profits solved. A decision made and acted upon. A person fired or hired, a needed vendor found and contracted with, a marketing campaign implemented. A sale made, a client acquired. **Here's a litmus test: accomplishment is always described presently in past tense.**

Conversely, activity includes things done that don't produce profits, but more so, things in progress moving along toward an uncertain end with an uncertain arrival time. Activity is a nagging or reccurring problem thought about, mulled over, discussed, handed off to a committee, or otherwise kept stewing. A decision unmade. Activity is always described presently in present or future tense.

The Lesson of My First Storyboard

The Storyboard is a time and task management tool that comes from moviemaking and has migrated into management largely thanks to the teaching and advocacy of Michael Vance, a close associate of Walt Disney's for a number of years. Mike uses it for what he calls "visual thinking." I like the device personally and have used it, off and on, over the years. To describe it in brief, it's a wall or other surface like a bulletin board, divided into three or four main columns: DO, DOING, and DONE or DO, DOING, DELEGATING, and DONE. Then ideas, items, and so on are written on little cards, displayed, moved around, and ultimately migrate to DONE.

The first time I set one up for myself was in 1979. It ran the entire length and height of a large wall in my office. I spent a lot of time getting it set up, for multiple major projects, each with a four-column layout. I had a bunch of items written out on little color-coded cards arranged on it. The same day I put the whole thing up, a very tough, grizzled veteran of managing companies in crisis, which is what I was doing at the time, dropped by my office at day's end to share a Scotch. (I drank at the time. A lot. And had a bottle of good Scotch at hand.) He surveyed my wall, asked a few questions about how it worked, and said, "You've got one thing really f***ed up here."

"What's that?" I asked grumpily, having spent all day on this work of art.

"Too damn much space for DOING, not near enough space for DONE."

He went on to say: "Most people allow too much space and time and have way too much tolerance for DOING in their businesses, in their days, with their people, and all that does is delay the DONE. You only get to pay the bills with DONE. If you got a lotta bills, you need a whole lotta DONE. And if you got a lotta unpaid bills, it just might be cuz you ain't got much DONE."

Ah-ha.

Don't Tell Me about the Labor Pains—Show Me the Baby

Recently I worked indepth with a fairly large and bureaucratically hamstrung corporate client on a major overhaul of its entire advertising, marketing, and sales efforts—a project targeted for completion in 4 months that dragged on painfully for more than 12. This is a rarity for me, and I became increasingly frustrated with the client and the 5-person team underneath the CEO who were responsible for implementation. The only real good news was that the CEO became increasingly frustrated with them instead of me. One day he asked me why I thought every little thing was taking so long. I said, "Because you are not holding any of these buffoons responsible for accomplishment. They are telling you what they are DOING, you are telling me what they're DOING, but nothing's ever DONE." Every day he was getting an update on the labor pains. But no baby ever popped out.

I realized early in my business life that the only way to get much DONE was to stop reveling in my labor pains and to refuse listening to others'. I first heard the axiom in a meeting in a client's office in 1976. I was waiting to discuss something with him. Two of his regional sales vice presidents were there, and one started to speak and got about eight words out when the President showed him his hand and yelled, "Stop. Just show me the baby and get the hell out of here. If you haven't got work to do, I do." I got the message about how this leader wanted to be communicated with, and, in fact, how really successful entrepreneurs need to be communicated with.

The Last and Most Important Lesson about This

A lot of activity has to do with attempting perfection or attempting mistake-proof, criticism-proof, ass-fully-covered, fail-safe implementation.

Some of this may be your fault. If you manage in a way that makes people fearful of making mistakes—rather than in a way that is focused on profitable Dones—then you are to blame. If you prize perfection and are thin-skinned about criticism, you are your business's worst enemy. I tell people that success gets cooked up in a messy kitchen. When you and/or your people are breaking new ground, it has to be OK for messes to be made, misfires to fizzle, and cleanups done on the run.

Bill Gates is, by most accounts, the richest man in the world. Has Microsoft *ever* released a completely debugged, perfect product? Apple sold more than 200,000 iPhones the first day knowing AT&T could never possibly get everybody's service turned on, but confident the frustrated consumers' grumbling and media reporting about it would not be enough to dampen the carefully orchestrated demand for its new, hot, and imperfect product. These companies separate getting to market and racking up huge sales as one Done, fixing the product as another Done.

DONE prematurely, even badly, is almost always more profitable than DOING, DOING, DOING, endlessly DOING and never DONE.

Every cent of my personal wealth and business's success has infinitely more to do with speed than with perfection. I know how easy it is for worthwhile projects to die in the Doing, so I'm eager to get them Done in a first version, not exactly right, certain to warrant later improvement, and get them launched, out the door, into the marketplace. The world that I and most of my clients live in would be very troubling to by-the-textbook MBAs. In fact, I have one client, the CEO of a franchise company, who admits his MBA is his worst enemy, because he's been conditioned to do things sequentially while we do things simultaneously. Our world is full of 24-, 36-, and 48-hour launches of new products that bring in a million dollars or more before the product is done. Our world is about managing chaos, not creating order. It's a hard thing for people who come from traditional academic and corporate environments to wrap their heads around. Not everybody can handle it. So beware the great resume; it may represent somebody who'd be great in a conventionally run corporation but unable to function in a high-performance, high-accomplishment entrepreneurial environment.

Being Unflinchingly Accomplishment Oriented

The cliché is "Leadership is top down." I suppose it's true. Certainly you set the tone for what goes on around you—or at least you should. The people working for you and around you should be strongly influenced by you, not the reverse. I think the best thing you can exhibit is an unflinchingly accomplishment-oriented attitude. If you cut every DOING conversation short and demand to either see a DONE or be left alone so at least you can be productive, people will get the idea.

Be sure you've got that space on your actual or figurative storyboard allocated correctly!

Vincent Palko
www.AdToons.com

CHAPTER 36

The Speed Imperative

Faster than a speeding bullet, leaps tall buildings in a single bound . . .

—THE GREATEST DESCRIPTIVE LINES EVER WRITTEN FOR A SUPERHERO

I'm a Jack Welch fan, despite the fact that I think he blathers on too much about "leadership." You can't argue with the facts of his accomplishments while at General Electric. And, underneath the "leadership talk," there's a tough-minded, demanding, aggressive guy all about progress and profit.

One of the things Jack brought to GE was an understanding of the need for speed. He took over a big, bloated, bureaucratic, and therefore horribly slow-moving creature with the determination to trim it, whip it into shape, and make it faster. He talked a lot about "the penalty for hesitation in the marketplace." Today, that penalty is much greater than it was when Jack remade GE. If you are slow today, by the time you get there, the rewards are all gone.

Just about everybody I've ever met in business frequently has good ideas. CEO's of big companies, owners of small companies, solo entrepreneurs, and my own peers in the information-marketing field, like authors, speakers, conference promoters, and publishers. All these good ideas are useless and valueless until they are DONE. Compressing the time between idea and action, and between action and completion, is where all the profit is.

I have a friend, for example, who came up with a truly outstanding idea for a book virtually certain to be a bestseller, land her on *Oprah,* and make her famous and richer than she already is. But she's working on (Doing) the book. Now, months after the idea. I don't think she grasps the Speed Imperative. The idea is very vulnerable during each minute it is incomplete. First of all, there are at least one million other people coming up with ideas for new books, including authors of previous bestsellers with agents and publisher relationships, hour by hour. There are a lot fewer slots for new books each year than there are new books being pitched to publishers. The likelihood of her being the only one with this idea is slim. The question is: Will somebody else get to completion first—a deal, a book done, a book in the market in the same space, in her way?

Second, ideas have a way of losing their power as their owners lose passion and enthusiasm for them over time. They sort of dissipate. If you have an idea that you'd like to own a little farm 50 miles or so outside of town and be a weekend farmer, it's much, much, much, much more likely to EVER happen in your life if you run out there the very first weekend the thought occurs to you and buy one even if you overpay and even if you're not ready than if you wait and ponder and wait and ponder. Or, if you feel a need to be a bit more prudent and methodical, you can at least set a relatively short time frame to get a farm bought and, that first weekend, bolt yourself away with all the information you can assemble, build the complete to-do list in steps, assign completion times to each step, list obstacles to overcome and people to find, build the whole plan, and implement at least some of it first thing Monday morning. Like hiring a real estate agent to find you a farm. My attitude is that you can always stop a project once started, but completing a project not started is pretty much impossible. So, if my friend were really serious, she'd have cleared her calendar for a week immediately upon falling in love with the idea, sent her husband packing, and gotten to work. Not necessarily writing the book, but doing all the research into what's out there in that category, shopping for the right agent, developing the book proposal, and so forth. All business projects and initiatives are the same as this book project. At the beginning they are nothing more than ideas with potential. Napoleon Hill, author of *Think and Grow Rich,* was not completely truthful when he stated, "Thoughts are things." Most thoughts are just fleeting thoughts; most projects never exit the womb. Thoughts certainly have the potential to be things *if* quickly and decisively acted on.

I'm very pleased that the person I work with most these days, Bill Glazer, the President of Glazer-Kennedy Insider's Circle™, has this approach and is willing to put things into motion before ready, start multiple projects simultaneously, recognizing only some of them will succeed, and push everybody around him for speed. Most of my clients work this way, too, and I'm continually ridding myself of those who don't.

Jack Welch told everybody at GE that "speed is EVERYTHING. It is THE indispensable ingredient in competitiveness."

At GE, he earned the nickname Neutron Jack for blowing up all the middle management levels he saw slowing things down. He streamlined and simplified communication, delegated authority even to dangerous extremes, and got rid of 10% to 20% of the entire work force by rote each year, continually culling the slow ones from the herd. Maybe most important and least understood tactic was that he launched many, many new initiatives simultaneously rather than sequentially. This is a key principle I emphasize in my Renegade Millionaire System®. It's contrary to your entire upbringing and conditioning; you've been incessantly warned that "haste makes waste" and taught to do things "one step at a time," not "all steps at the same time." But that's not how accomplishment *really* happens, not how entrepreneurial wealth is *really* created.

Recommended Resource #8

Information about the Renegade Millionaire System® is available at www.RenegadeMillionaire.com. The System incorporates strategies in common from several hundred first-generation, from-scratch millionaire, multimillionaire, and seven-figure-income entrepreneurs I've worked with indepth for many years. The experience-based strategies encompass marketing, management, entrepreneurship, and wealth.

It's easier to understand this if in a turnaround situation with a troubled company. If Iacocca had approached Chrysler's troubles pedantically and sequentially, he'd have first made cuts in operations, *then* worked on financial restructuring, *then* turned his attention to improvements in the product line and new products, *then* developed better advertising and better offers for consumers—and by then, there would have been no Chrysler. I was at a little meeting at Lee Iacocca's house in Palm Desert, California, when somebody asked him if he could list the steps he took to turn around Chrysler in order. "Order?" he huffed contemptuously. "There was no order. We did it all at once." And at the speed of light.

Iacocca simultaneously put two new products on the road with virtually no research, restructured financing, sold the government and banks on a bailout, cut fat, changed pricing, boldly offered consumers a new, better warranty with no earthly way of predicting its future cost, and took on the spokesperson role to sell his cars and his company to consumers himself. Jack Welch said he tried to infuse GE with a "small-business soul" so it "could be run like a corner grocery store." Iacocca pretty much ran Chrysler like a corner grocery store or at least like an entrepreneur running his own small business. In a much smaller but comparably pressured turnaround situation, I honed my own "simultaneous, not sequential" approach and skills; then I reasoned, if this works with a horribly troubled company barely escaping extinction day by day, under this kind of extreme pressure, imagine how well it can work in better circumstances! To this day, I look at every business as a turnaround situation.

Ironically, many small-business owners operate what should be agile little speedboats as if they were gigantic freighters, even while the savviest CEOs who inherit big, sluggish freighters try remaking them into flotillas of agile speedboats.

To manage for maximum profit—and survival—today, you must bring the Speed Imperative into your business. The Speed Imperative is a philosophy and an attitude, an overriding idea of how your business is to be operated, that has to be crystallized in your own mind, embraced emotionally, and communicated to everybody around you, relentlessly. This, more than anything else, is what Jack Welch brought to GE, and it's what you can bring to your business. The Speed Imperative is then applied in practical ways in many different aspects of your business, from marketing to innovation to testing new strategies to expansion.

Recommended Resource #9

I've developed an indepth "special report" covering the ten biggest overlooked or hidden opportunities in businesses best leveraged for new profits with Speed Imperative Strategies. If you would like a copy free of charge, you can go to www.NoBSBooks.com, click the "MANAGEMENT BOOK" icon, then click the "SPEED REPORT" icon.

With all this said about speed, I'd be remiss if I skipped the two big caveats.

Caveat 1: Everything, every relationship is easier to get into than to get out of. Never go in anywhere without a predetermined escape route. Never enter any relationship without a prenegotiated exit. Prenups are infinitely easier to negotiate and infinitely less costly than are postnups. You will be tempted to ignore this advice with any number of justifications: *Bob and I have been buddies for 20 years . . . We have an understanding; there's no need to bother with a lot of paperwork and legal mumbo jumbo . . . I don't want to offend him* . . . yadda, yadda. Each and every one of these justifications is unjustified. Each time I've made this dumb mistake (hey, only three times in 30 years), it's been very expensive and troublesome. I have had to pay somebody I'd been buddies with a lot of money just to go away at a time I could least afford it. I have gone through a very costly divorce without a prenup. No need to bore you with the details.

Caveat 2: Don't be afraid to reverse yourself and kill a project or get out of a business situation as soon as you determine, for whatever reason, that it is more trouble than it's worth. A little egg on your face now is preferable to a 1,000-pound anchor chained to your ankle while in shark-infested waters later. Never stay in a bad or deteriorating or unreasonably dangerous situation out of ego. You need to be just as fast in reverse as you are in forward.

CHAPTER 37

How to Ruthlessly Manage a Rapidly Growing Business

BY CHRIS HURN

When Dan initially asked me to write this chapter, I was hesitant since I don't normally openly state that my management style is "ruthless." I've generally kept that to myself and only a handful of others who I know can appreciate the nuances. Ironically, with 951% top-line growth year over year in the past three years (landing us on the 2007 *Inc. Magazine*'s 500 list of fastest-growing private firms in America) and, more importantly, net profit growth in the quadruple-digit percentages over that time period, I've lost only two employees I considered "key" at the time of their departure (when you're a visible, fast-growing, innovative company, plenty of vultures will try to poach your people; some strategies for dealing with that follow). The rest of my employees remain quite happy, even anonymously voting us one of the finalists for "Best Places to Work" in Orlando by our local business journal for the past three years running. So how have I done it, while being ruthless, you ask? Great question. Here's a summary of how I did it and how I still do it.

Profits Trump People

I've always found it interesting how some folks will argue for the abolition of a strong military in their defense of and presumed substitution of "peace." What these same people fail to understand is that a meaningful peace is impossible if a country cannot defend itself and survive against its enemies. No means of defense eventually equals no country, which also eventually means no peace.

Companies are no different than countries as it relates to their necessary survival philosophies. Instead of having a military, profits are the means by which a company protects itself and survives long term. Without them, any company will shrivel and die. Therefore, putting profits above all other things is a fundamental principle in understanding how to run a successful company.

Even a fast-growing company will eventually have to turn a profit if it is to survive in the long run. Like it or not, companies do not serve, in their primary focus, as employment "guarantors." The critics that argue putting profits above people is the cornerstone of "ruthless management" are right, and I don't choose to view it as an insult one bit. Those same people fail to understand that without eventual profits, there can be no companies, which means there can be no jobs for anyone. If job cutting is what really bothers them, oftentimes that's just a temporary Band-Aid® solution to strategy gone awry and a lack of free-market economic understanding. The profits (the results of a properly run business's activities) are really all that matters. If understanding this fundamental economic reality is a hallmark to having a ruthless management philosophy, then count me in.

Crusading for Your Cause

To properly grow a successful business, it takes a team approach—you will be limited if you try to do everything yourself. The collaborative efforts of individuals on a team are always stronger than the sum of its individual parts. And your team will need to have a very clear sense of the business's priorities, what you really stand for as an organization, to be truly effective.

Unlike so many me-too companies, our innovative firm brings a genuine value to our target audience that previously was lacking—we formed our company not to pursue some hobby or childhood passion, but because we identified a clear gap in the marketplace to exploit and fill. We completely upended the commercial banking model, shattered the existing norms and ripped up the conventions, and we haven't looked back since. We're still the underdog in our industry, daily competing against plenty of Big, Dumb Companies, so we made it a bit of our "crusade" to educate owners of small and mid-sized businesses about our smarter financing options. We've disrupted the status quo in our industry with an insurgent mentality, and it is the key differentiator in attracting our customers.

You will have to instill a sense of mission into all your employees, ideally beginning on their hire dates. Everyone involved will need to have a laserlike focus on what the most critical components are that drive your business higher and produce the results (profits) that truly matter. Nothing can be allowed to deter you and your team from these goals. It's about having a cause—nothing short of that—and this keeps everyone aligned.

Your job as a leader will be to set this guiding vision and to get your people buying into it—yes, you *will* have to sell and resell them on this until they will walk through walls for you. You cannot expect your people to dedicate themselves to the cause if you cannot make them easily understand the "why" and "how" they directly contribute to it. You'll have to directly link the strategic imperatives for them to become emotionally vested.

Instilling your core values that reflect your overall mission into all of your employees gives them the fortitude to stomach many of the other keys to growth. Properly done, your employees are working for something much greater than just you and themselves. One way to do this is to think of your firm's fiscal year like it's on an election cycle, and each "primary" win is another one to celebrate on your way to the big, yearly contest.

As the leader of your company, it is your responsibility to consistently put forth the vision and hitch your employees' wagons to it. They've got to head in the same direction as you, or they shouldn't be your employees anymore. Some won't like it . . . but who's paying whom, after all? It's your company, so you've got to be a benevolent dictator. It's really that simple.

Focus Is Freeing

All fast-growing companies are by definition speedy and flexible. They're more agile and lean than the incumbents in their industry, or they won't maintain their fast growth for long. A tenacious focus on what you can do and cannot do is one of the most powerful things a business can ever maintain. You cannot be all things to all people, as the adage goes. Saying no more often will paradoxically make you more successful by keeping you focused on your core strategy and positioning you better as a specialist in what you do best. It can be very liberating, but it will take courage to reject perfectly good business that doesn't quite fit.

Far too many companies lose focus when they try to do too much. Oftentimes when a company is accused of growing too fast and outstripping its resources, it is because it got off track and tried to do too many things that weren't synergistically linked to its primary goals. You've got to have the ruthless discipline to stay unwaveringly on task. Clarity creates competence; competence creates confidence; and confidence aids your positioning and eventually your profits. And, inspired employees work harder, accomplish more, and are happier being part of an entity that is striving toward its full potential. The relentless focus on your crusade and your competitive advantages embeds itself in your corporate DNA—pretty soon your top people will be disapprovingly telling *you* when another employee won't drink the Kool-Aid®.

Enable Emerging Entrepreneurs

As the nation's only commercial lender that always leads with the best commercial loan product for owners of small and midsized firms purchasing or constructing their own commercial real estate, we are proud supporters of America's entrepreneurs and their smarter wealth creation through our little-known commercial loan product. From day one, I've instilled in each of my employees a desire to have their own enterprises someday. I've told them repeatedly that they need to absorb all the business lessons they can at our small, fast-growing company, so they'll be better prepared to successfully run their own firm one day. Some would think that this kind of empowerment would merely lead to them leaving me sooner, but I find exactly the opposite occurs. They're emboldened to not just work here but learn here and do better, more innovative work here. We work at developing this entrepreneurial spirit in all of our employees so that decisions can be made quickly at all levels. This fosters more speed while breeding more accountability.

Routinely pushing decision-making responsibilities back toward my employees gives them more autonomy and saves me time. It doesn't do any of them any good if I make all of the decisions ALL of the time. Sometimes they'll make mistakes, but that's just fine, as I never want to punish people for taking smart, calculated risks. A lack of the pursuit of excellence is a far greater sin in my company. If you want to be innovative, you're going to have to take risks and experiment and test. This means you'll deal with failures regularly or, as I like to think of them, obstacles to be overcome. Minor failures are merely learning opportunities, but the important thing is that we're taking action—most don't. You can't set the pace of innovation in your industry without constantly testing the edges of the possible.

We're very open about communicating almost everything with our employees, and my business partner and I are both frustrated, wanna-be teachers, so we enjoy connecting the dots regularly for our troops. We've created a culture of responsibility and authority down to every level in our firm, where people are responsible not only for generating revenue but also for watching expenses. Lots of fast-growing companies forget the latter in their hell-bent pursuit of growth simply for growth's sake. Sure, we've had a setback or two, but when we did, we quickly assembled the team in a huddle to discuss the temporary small blip on our course to success and optimizing profits.

As a part-time business coach to other business owners, I apply many of the same tactics to my employees as I do my coaching clients: challenging; stimulating; encouraging; and invigorating. At my firm, we have fostered the value of ongoing performance improvement. But I also use the power of Andrew Carnegie and Napoleon Hill's Mastermind Principle to my advantage regularly. As an example of this, for nearly three years now, I host twice-a-month "reading meetings" over lunch, where I buy and a different employee each time presents and summarizes a famous business book for the rest of us.

That same employee is then expected to facilitate discussion in an effort to reflect and relate important points back to our company—what we're doing right, what we're doing wrong, and what we *need* to be doing. We spare no one from this exercise, not even our interns. This allows the entire firm to share in the knowledge from these books, while the employees gain practice presenting, defending ideas, and managing a meeting. And of course, it's a quick way to disseminate information most people would have a hard time getting through in several years' time. It also subtly forces our people to view work as more than just a place to earn a paycheck and demonstrates to them that learning is a lifelong experience. All of this is part of a very deliberate learning culture I've crafted in our business since I first came to appreciate one when I worked at GE Capital for a number of years while Jack Welch was still the CEO.

We work at developing the best skill sets of our employees so they can readily absorb the challenges that come with growth and also make better judgments. This accomplishes the development of their full potential, and this entrepreneurial attitude also rubs off on our prospective clients, too, especially since so many of my employees are actual employee-owners with an ownership stake in our company. I often half-joke that I'll need something to do eventually if we ever sell our business, and sitting on my former employees' corporate boards sounds like just the kind of relaxing, yet engaged thing for me to spend my retirement time doing. It'll sure be more stimulating than chasing a silly white ball around some lovely landscaping for days on end.

Handle Chaos and Honor Change

If you're growing, and I mean *actually accomplishing something*, chaos will always be there. You can't make an omelet without breaking some eggs, as they say. Forced patience and a tolerance for ambiguity and uncertainty are necessary skills if you're going to lead a fast-growing firm. No one actually likes chaos; we just accept it better. And if that weren't enough, there's no point in resisting change, either, since that's a constant. This is enough to give me a healthy sense of paranoia and to have essentially replaced myself in my company in all areas except for overall strategy and marketing so I can better prepare us to handle what'll be happening next. Oh and lest you think I'm slipping in some way, I still walk around the office at least once every day to check in with every employee to find out what he's up to and how he's doing. That regular touch is an important managerial tool for fast-growing companies.

Another way to better handle chaos and change is to systematize every process and best practice. This allows for better decisions that are quickly executed with fewer ad hoc decisions. Our ability to execute faster than our competition is all related to us ruthlessly making things more efficient and simple, while constantly looking for better ways to do what is currently being done. We relentlessly monitor a small number of performance measurements (leave all the extraneous ratios to ordinary bankers) to evaluate, analyze, and improve efficiencies even more.

Many think you can't have discipline in a fast-growing environment without killing the entrepreneurial spirit, but that's a fallacy. You *must* have it. Discipline is the fundamental key for executing on the right things at the right time in the right way.

Hire Blank Slates and Winners, Not Whiners

I hire for attitude and work ethic first, knowledge and skills second. We've never hired anyone who previously worked in our industry—never. In that way (which is heresy in our industry), we get people with no baggage whom we can train in *our* ways. We hire young, energetic, creative, and boundlessly curious people, and that allows us to assimilate information and expertise very quickly. They don't know what they don't know, so they try new things and apply things from other industries to our own. I used to do this when I was a management consultant—apply what was working in other industries successfully to one of my clients in another industry—and I cultivate this type of behavior in our people. We certainly have never had the "not-invented-here" syndrome at our company. I've hired six of our full-timers from our intern pool, and for two-thirds of our employees, our company is the very first real-world job experience they've ever had.

Exploiting people's will to win is fundamentally useful, too. Successful people want to be with other successful people—like attracts like in this case. It's a thrill to accomplish wins on the battlefield as corporate athletes. The best talent wants to work for the best companies, so performance, vision, and culture are the best ways to get the top talent. Plenty of others can try to duplicate our culture, but at the end of the day, they can't copy our talented individuals, who are our primary draws. When you ruthlessly hire correctly, that can be your advantage, too.

Final Thoughts

You can be "ruthless" at the same time that you're being respectful. They aren't mutually exclusive terms. When you're ruthless, oftentimes you're merely being straightforward with people. They'll call it ruthless when they don't agree with what you've stated . . . but they'll call it some variation of just "telling it like it is" when they *do* agree. Perhaps my Midwestern upbringing just molded me into thinking that honesty, even when it's brutal, is always the best policy.

If asked about who their best coaches or teachers were, most people will name their toughest one. It will be the one who was the most demanding and expected constant progress; the one who wouldn't *let you* fail yourself. Being ruthless doesn't mean being brutish or nasty, just firm in knowing where you're taking your people and the business . . . and that optimization of profits is what counts.

How compassionate are you really being when you're quietly dishonest toward an employee who doesn't fit in, isn't meaningfully contributing to the company's goals, or isn't living up to his full and obvious potential, by just leaving him in a dead-end job (you won't *really* be promoting him, will you?)? Isn't it far better for you, your company, and the employee to honestly tell him it isn't working and give him constructive feedback so he can take corrective action within a set period of time or leave your firm altogether?

Coddling employees will kill a company. They don't need another parent; they need a leader, a boss that will teach them everything he knows, hold them accountable, and make them better businesspeople for the company's benefit as well as for their own. You show them you care by being tough when you need to be. To do otherwise is to act like those teachers that keep "caring" so much about the illiterate students that they keep advancing them to higher grades—it hurts all parties involved.

So who's ready to become a modern-day John Galt with me? If that reference is lost on you, go buy Ayn Rand's book *Atlas Shrugged* IMMEDIATELY for more inspiration.

CHRIS HURN is President of Mercantile Commercial Capital (MCC), the nation's leading 90% loan-to-cost commercial loan provider. His firm has been named to the *Inc.* magazine's 500 list of fastest-growing private companies in America, and he has been named the "Banker of the Year" by his industry's only trade association, was named the "Marketing Guru of the Year" by Coleman Publishing, and was the Small Business Administration's Financial Services Champion of the Year for Florida and for the 12-state Southeast region. Visit www.504Experts.com, call (866) 622-4504, or e-mail info@mercantilecc.com for more information.

CHAPTER 38

How They Should Communicate with You

Executives who get there and stay suggest solutions when they present problems.

—Malcolm Forbes

The number-one complaint I have about people and always had about my employees, and that I hear from my clients about their employees, is they can't communicate.

The complaint has validity. Generally, people have no idea how to communicate effectively and efficiently. Enormous time gets wasted. Here's an example: I called one of my two CPAs, got his voice mail, and left this exact message: "I need to know when you will have my Kennedy Sports Corporation tax work done so I can tell the other CPA when to expect it. Call and tell me."

Here's the message he left me in return: "I'm working on the taxes. Call me if you have any questions."

Did I have any questions? Well, yes I did. The same one I called with the first damned time that he didn't answer. Aaaargh. And this sort of thing goes on all the time. In my case, I cut down on it a lot in three ways. First, I try very hard to train people in how they should communicate with me. Second, I try very hard to eliminate people from my life who prove unable or unwilling to learn how to communicate with me as I want to be communicated with. Three, I rarely engage in telephone communication like the above fruitless exercise with the accountant at all; I force people to communicate with me in writing by fax, never e-mail, which forces them to stop and think and be coherent. I communicate with everybody the same way.

For your purposes, let's talk about the first remedy, the training.

How to Communicate with You about Problems

I once had 47 employees in a troubled company environment where there was some sort of crisis every hour on the hour. I gradually trained the people I kept not to bring me a new problem without simultaneously bringing me the basic information I needed to make an intelligent decision plus at least three possible solutions. That template looked like the one in Figure 37.1.

When you force people into a process like this, you accomplish quite a bit. First of all, it stops people from bursting into your office screaming or sending you a hysterical and incomprehensible e-mail. Second, it forces the person with the problem to actually think about it before he can dump it in your lap or anybody else's. If they're worth having around at all, they'll wind up deciding on a solution and handling the whole matter on their

FIGURE **37.1:** Problem-Solution Communication Template

Name of Problem or Crisis: ____________________

Five Key Facts You Need to Know about It:

1. ____________________
2. ____________________
3. ____________________
4. ____________________
5. ____________________

Two Possible Solutions to Consider:

Solution 1 ____________________

Pros	Cons
________	________
________	________
________	________

Solution 2 ____________________

Pros	Cons
________	________
________	________
________	________

own some percentage of the time. Third, you can actually have an intelligent conversation about the problem and potential solutions if you must, instead of always having at least three or four consecutive conversations.

We also developed a code, sort of like Homeland Security's colorful terror alert thing. If you arrived with a problem, the first thing I asked you for was its numerical ranking, from 1 to 5. Five meant that life on this planet might end if it wasn't dealt with immediately. One meant that it was bugging you, but waiting a day or two to deal with it probably wouldn't matter much. After a while, people got that they had to accurately answer that question. This reduced the number of emergencies, led to more thinking on their part, and kept me from committing suicide. I should mention that, at the time, I was experimenting with the "open-door management" idea highly recommended in most of the management books I'd hurriedly consumed when I woke up with all these employees. And if there's a dumber management idea, it'd be amusing to see it. You might want a glass door so you can see 'em and they know you can, but you'll still want to shove a really heavy couch in front of it to keep them out.

The point is not so much whether you like this specific technique or any other I might use or recommend. The point is that you need a set way that you permit employees and vendors to communicate with you that works best for you. You may have one method or different methods for different situations or even for different people. Whatever works best for you. Think of it as a little instruction manual for communicating with you: *The Care and Feeding of Information to the Boss.* The point is that you teach it to everybody who has to communicate with you and get them to use it.

But what if they won't follow your instructions?

Step 1: Off to remedial reading class they go. You refuse to accept their communications if presented in a noncompliant way. You gently say, "Sorry, but that's not how I take in information. Good-bye." Maybe you hand them another copy of your little instruction manual. Under no circumstances—unless you can actually see the place on fire behind them as they are yelling "Fire!"—do you permit them to ignore your instructions. Not once. No exceptions. Rebuff them. Send them away. Hang up on them.

Step 2: If Step 1 fails, forget gentle. Sit them down and read them the riot act.

Step 3: Fired. Next. I promise, you will wind up with people who can follow directions eventually, if you insist on it.

CHAPTER 39

How to Hold Meetings

The Law of Meetings: There's an inverse relationship between the number of people in a meeting and what will be accomplished.

—Dr. Gene Landrum, founder of Chuck E. Cheese Pizza; author of *Profiles of Power* and *Entrepreneurial Genius*

In the May 2007 issue of GQ Magazine, writer Cecil Donahue said this: "Nothing crushes the soul—or your productivity—like a day full of meetings . . . pure torture. Not only a wearying time suck, but also a double whammy: every minute wasted in mind-numbing boredom was also a minute lost attacking the various stacks on my desk." He went on to describe the people most often found populating the endless meetings everybody seems to be in whenever you call a company. Included, some from his list, some from mine, are the following individuals:

- **The Bloviator**. He has an MBA and wants to be sure you know it. *Tick-tock, there goeth the clock.*

- **The Merry Quipster**. A little fun's fine. But he thinks the meeting's being held in a comedy club. *Tick-tock, tick-tock, around your neck a rock.*
- **The Yes-Men and Brown-Nosers**. Since they are bobble-head clones of the boss, they are an entire waste of time, air, and doughnuts. *Tick-tock, tick-tock, tick-tock, the urge to gag as great as if, in your mouth, a sock.*
- **The Killer**. He's never met an idea he doesn't hate and can't come up with 402 reasons it won't work. *Tick-tock, shoot the clock.*
- **The Mover**. He prevents any decisions or resolution of anything in favor of more research, committees formed, items tabled for future meetings, and more meetings scheduled for items tabled. *Tick-tocks, roadblocks.*
- **Mr. Meetings.** The worst of all. The boss or project manager, who loves the sound of his own voice, loves hearing what a genius he is, secretly loves pitting people against each other, loves avoiding any real work, loves covering his ass with groupthink he can later blame for anything that goes wrong (while taking full credit for anything that goes right), and most of all, loves those little deli sandwiches. *Tick-tock, tick-tock, tick-tock, tick-tock, sell your stock.*

It's up to you to prevent this B.S. from taking over your company.

The Best Meeting May Be No Meeting

The first thing to do is to avoid having all these meetings in the first place. There are other options for collecting input and disseminating information. For example, posing a question to people and making each one respond separately in writing forces them to think; avoids emotions linked to interpersonal conflicts and jockeying for position from coloring the input; eliminates all the time consumed by bloviating, joke telling, arguing; and gives you something you can quietly consider, say while being driven home by your chauffer or sitting on the can. Improves everybody's productivity.

If you can't cut out a meeting, consider cutting down on the people in it. Not everybody with two cents to offer or a need to know needs to be there. Some can contribute in advance in writing; some can be informed after the fact.

If You Feed 'Em, They Might Move In

The second thing to do: stop feeding them. Another consultant and I used to love joining one company's employees at their lengthy new product brainstorming meetings because the food was just outstanding. On arrival, five different kinds of bagels, flavored cream cheeses, doughnuts, fruit, imported cheeses. Only a couple hours later, lunch! Little deli sandwiches with the crusts cut off, gourmet potato salad, fresh veggies and dips. In the afternoon, bakery (not grocery store) cookies, brownies, and miniature cream puffs. If this guy had added masseuses giving shoulder massages, we'd still be there. Of course, we were also getting paid our hefty daily fees. But for the employees it was a soul-draining, mind-numbing, woefully unproductive experience just as the *GQ* writer described his. Productive people hate these things. Unproductive people love 'em. You can reduce their appeal by taking away the food.

You can further reduce the appeal of minimeetings by making them stand-up meetings. At the very least, resist the urge to create a Taj Mahal conference room with plush, comfortable chairs. Decorate with clocks.

Insist on Outcomes

The third thing you can do is actually manage the meeting. Have a preset agenda with defined objectives, time pre-allocated by topic, and the decision to occur by meeting's end predefined. Participants need to know the meeting has a purpose.

Vincent Palko
www.AdToons.com

CHAPTER 40

Friendly as Long as You Feed Them

Sooner or later you sleep in your own space.

—Billy Joel, "My Life"

As the owner of a business, ultimately you are **alone**. You may have a hundred employees around you, you may get nice gift baskets from your vendors, you may be the local hero at the Chamber meeting, you may even be famous to your peers in your industry or profession. Never let any of that fool you. Let something negative and cataclysmic happen, and you'll find nearly all of these folks gone missing.

At least once every summer, there's a story in the news about some numb-nut in a national park who sits on a ledge tossing jelly doughnuts to a couple bears. The bears happily eat the treats and behave like big, friendly dogs. Until the idiot runs out of doughnuts. Then the bears eat the idiot. This is a useful thinning of the herd, but it's also a true and accurate representation of how most employees behave. Friendly as long as you feed them.

In one of the early Presidential debates in 2007, Rudy Giuliani was struggling to explain his pro-life/pro-abortion position when electric shocks came through the microphone, mimicking lightning. He quipped that such a thing was frightening to somebody who'd gone to parochial schools. The other candidates joked by all moving steps away from him. Well, that's exactly what goes on in real business life when things go awry. Ask Martha Stewart or Arnold Taubman how quickly people distanced themselves when they were arrested, prosecuted, publicly pilloried, and sent off to jail. Ask Donald Trump to compare the numbers of people eager to be around him at the height of his *Apprentice*-fueled popularity with those who showed up during the years he spent teetering on the brink of bankruptcy.

Given that this is true—and it is—you must ultimately, always do what you judge to be in *your* best interest. You have to give yourself full permission to do that, no qualms, no strings attached.

A few years ago, I had a confrontation in a meeting with the account executive representing a prospective client's current ad agency. I made a simple suggestion: He could put up $50,000.00 out of his pocket to run the ad he'd prepared against the one I'd prepared, which I'd run with $50,000.00 out of my pocket. Whoever won would get $50,000.00 from the other, and be reimbursed by the client for the $50,000.00 spent running the superior ad. The loser would eat his ad cost and pay the winner. He sputtered like an old, bad lawn mower running on politically correct ethanol. He was insulted by the unprofessional nature of my proposal. And, of course, he wanted no part of the wager.

This is the way it is. Every single day, you, the business owner, put yourself at risk. The others who disapprove of your actions put nothing at risk.

Everybody has lots of opinions, but hardly anybody is willing to put himself on the line to accept consequential responsibility for them. Lots of people are willing to privately and publicly pass judgment on you, your decisions, your business practices, but few will offer to open up their own checkbooks to wager on being right. It's also very important to keep in mind that most people expressing opinions, generously offering you their wise counsel free of charge, and gifting their criticisms have their own agendas—some practical, some emotional.

Every employee thinks he's smarter than the boss. Your employees think they are overworked and underpaid, making a much greater contribution to your business than you are, smarter than you are, and therefore well justified in ignoring or circumventing your directives, standards, and procedures. And should you be delusional about your business being some sort of all-for-one, one-for-all exception, try this experiment: call everybody in, tell them you just lost a major account or had some other economic reversal, announce that you're taking a 20% pay cut for an indeterminate length of time, and ask for volunteers to do the same. If you like, take it further and give everybody a day to privately let you know whether (1) he is willing to take that 20% pay cut to save everybody's jobs and keep the ship afloat or (2) he prefers keeping 100% of his pay and having others laid off. Unity will be in short supply.

Consider a U.S. automaker like General Motors, Ford, or Chrysler. I can't recall a month passing in recent years without the recall of thousands of cars with various manufacturing defects being announced. I had a new car with 7 different recalls in 18 months. When these occur, do you suppose all the employees who actually worked on these cars and put all the brake lines in backward or neglected to seal the moonroofs all come forward, march over to the CEO's office, and say, "Hey, my bad. Our screwup. Please dock our pay appropriately, so all the stockholders who've invested here with the perfectly reasonable expectation that we're going to be awake while assembling these cars don't suffer?" Does the head of the union call a press conference to announce the employees' eagerness to share responsibility for the recall costs, damage to the company's brand, and inconvenience or danger and harm to the customers?

Should you find anyone willing to book the bet, you may wager your life savings on this never happening in complete safety, with as much certainty as betting against Paris Hilton ever receiving an Oscar (or any other recognition of talent) or of Al Gore ever again using the word *lockbox*.

Profits of businesses are shared, by paying salaries, bonuses, and benefits to employees at every level, by paying taxes to local, state, and federal governments, by purchasing goods and services from vendors, by paying for advertising in media, and on and on. After all that profit sharing, you, the owner, get to keep whatever's left over. That might be about 2% of all the money if, say, you own supermarkets or certain kinds of industrial manufacturing companies. It might be as much as 20% if you own a professional practice or service business. Regardless, it's a long, long way from 100% of the money. But 100% of the responsibility is yours and yours alone. Don't ever lose sight of this fact.

This knowledge has to empower you. To think about yourself. To view your business as a means of achieving your personal goals. To always do what you judge to be in *your* best interest. You have to give yourself full permission to do that, no qualms, no strings attached. This flies in the face of plentiful advice about putting customers first and others' equally zealous advice about putting employees first. Nonsense. He who puts his chips on the table and neck in the noose every day gets priority.

One of the many objects I have in my office as reminders to myself is a miniature wooden hanging platform with a noose suspended from its top. It's prominently displayed on a bookshelf, to catch my eye and jog my memory, telling me it's my neck in the noose.

CHAPTER 41

Why I Can't Do These Things

The price of progress is trouble.

—Charles F. Kettering

The reasons business owners tell me they can't do the obviously, patently logical and sensible things described in this book include

1. My employees won't do it.
2. My employees won't accept this kind of environment.
3. Bertha (ONE employee) won't let me.
4. It's bad for morale.
5. It makes me look like a tyrant.
6. What will people think?
7. My business is different.
8. I don't have time for this kind of management.

Regarding excuses 1, 2, and 3: One of the saddest, most pitiful things I ever hear from business owners is "but my employees won't let me." I hear it a lot. It seems the inmates are running the asylums and the wardens have surrendered, north, east, south, and west. Of course, it is possible to present your new Program in such a negative, belligerent way that you spark mutiny—and deserve it. This does have to be *sold*. But it is also likely you are living in tyranny in your own business, and you really should stop. Employees are replaceable. Lost profits are not.

Regarding excuse 4: Morale is a funny thing. It's subjective and variable. While a definite Program and supervisory enforcement are hated and resented by some employees, it is welcomed by others. There are plenty of people who prefer working in an environment with strong leadership, good management, a well-defined Program, clearly defined opportunities and rewards and penalties, and elimination of bad employees around them. They actually want to do the work, do the work well, and have accurately measured accomplishment. Everything I've talked about here is absolutely awful for the morale of noncompliant, unprofitable employees. But you may be surprised at its effects on the morale of productive, profitable employees!

Regarding excuses 5 and 6: The only opinions that really matter are those of the customers, clients, or patients who make deposits to your bank account. I have two books to recommend on this issue of sensitivity to criticism, to be read in this order: *The New Psycho-Cybernetics,* which I co-authored with the late Dr. Maxwell Maltz, then *Thick Face, Black Heart* by Chin-Ning Chu. You need to read the first to be prepared for the second.

Regarding excuse 7: No, it isn't.

Regarding excuse 8: If you decide to put a small herd of cattle in your backyard, you'd damn well better make time to feed them, water them, care for them, and constantly repair your fences. If you are going to have employees, they come with a collection of responsibilities. If you are going to have profitable employees, these responsibilities cannot be ignored.

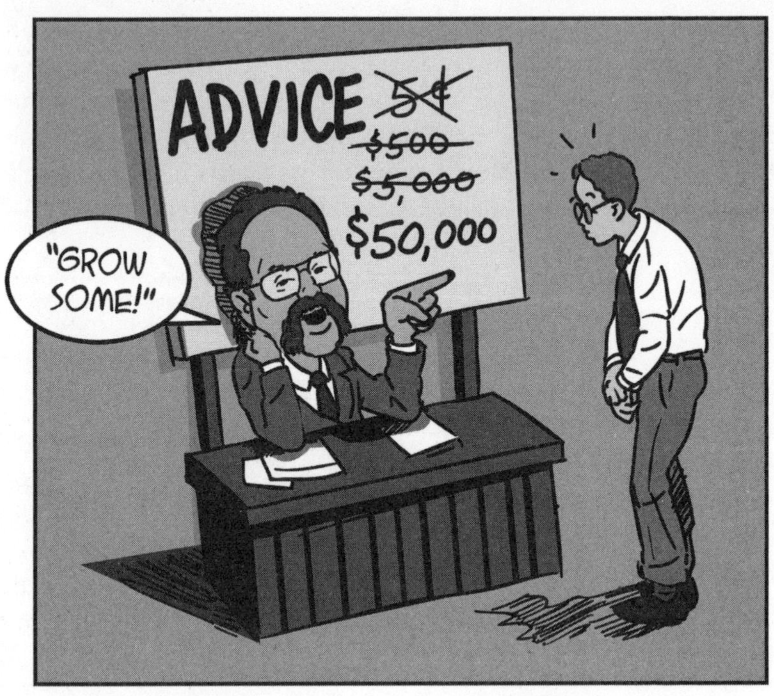

Vincent Palko
www.AdToons.com

CHAPTER 42

What Is "Profit," Anyway?

A company's No. 1 responsibility is not to the customer but to the shareholder. It doesn't mean that the customer isn't important. But the people who invest in a company own it— not the employees, not the suppliers, not the customers, and not the community.

—Albert Dunlap, turnaround wizard and author of *Mean Business: How I Save Bad Companies and Make Good Companies Great*

Accountants can make fabulously unprofitable companies seem profitable. Enron leaps to mind, but almost every quarter, some big company is "restating its earnings." A lot of small-business owners are similarly confused. I've certainly had clients who couldn't differentiate between gross and net. Since this is a book about managing for profit, I thought it might be worth a stab at definition.

There are different kinds of profit.

One is the amount of money that you, the owner, remove from the business in cash as yours. This might include your salary, bonuses, contributions to your retirement accounts, and health benefits. It might also include the salaries paid to your wife, mistress, unemployable brother-in-law you'd have to support anyway, and that "fact-finding junket" you went on to Las Vegas. You need to be reasonably honest with yourself about all this, or you may be unhappy without just cause. One client complained to me that he was only keeping $300,000.00 a year from his $3 million business. Quizzed, he wasn't counting $100,000.00 put into his retirement accounts, a large low-interest loan he was using to invest in very profitable real estate, rental payments he got from his company for his vacation home and boat when he hosted meetings there, and, of course, the salary paid to his unemployable brother-in-law he'd have to support anyway.

On the other hand, it's important not to fool yourself either. The fact that your business rented your vacation home or bought you first-class tickets to Vegas, where you did drop in on a trade show, well, that's nice. But it's still money that's gone altogether or disappeared into an asset like your vacation home or boat that may have questionable future worth as an investment. In short, there's "total net profit" and then there's "net cash profits, retained." It's this second number, "net cash profit, retained," that matters most, because this is the only number that can translate into financial security for you and your family.

I firmly believe it's a mistake to let all or most of your wealth accumulate and be tied up in your business, for the dreamt-about day when some big, dumb company or deep-pocketed investor will arrive to buy you out at a nice multiple of all that accumulated value. A business is a thing to take money out of. A business owner must measure his success, in large part, by the amount of the gross that runs through his hands that he is able to get out of the business and into untouchable and reasonably secure investments, such as cash in Federal Deposit Insurance Corporation (FDIC)-insured banks, top-rated bonds, and real estate in stable markets. Most business owners err in thinking they'll take care of such things "later." They should be done from day one, done every day, week, or month, every pay day. This all-important number should be managed and made to grow on a schedule.

The other type of profit is equity.

Equity can be confusing, too. A lot of what gets put on balance sheets and counted as accumulating equity actually has diminishing and little or no cash value to the business owner if and when he needs to borrow against it or goes to sell the business. I bought a company once that had more than $3 million of a particular so-called asset on its balance sheet, certified as worth exactly that by a famous-name Big-Eight Accounting Firm. However, this asset had value only to the business as it was operated and lost value with age rapidly—a loss never calculated by the accountants. As a practical matter, the asset was worth somewhere between $0.00 and about $50,000.00 for the raw material. This is really quite common. Owners con themselves, accountants confuse them, and owners and accountants lie to stupid bankers about these things.

An asset is worth only what it could be sold for, today.

If you have, for example, a building full of perfectly functional equipment you're happy to use but that has been antiquated by two newer generations of technology, it is not worth the million dollars you paid for it less your accountant's formulaic depreciation. It's worth only what you could get for it today at auction, with an ad in the paper, or on eBay. If you have, for example, a half million dollars in inventory you carry, but it's useful only in the products you make, and they're only useful providing your chief account keeps buying them, you do not have a half million dollars. You have hope worth a penny, plus whatever the raw material would sell for as is, today, on the auction block. This is why I've always said that inventory is evil.

However, there is an asset that gets short shrift on balance sheets, that is worth much more than any bean-counter formula allows, that you should be aggressively investing in acquiring and nurturing: customers and good, active relationships with them.

Buildings burn down. Locations go from great to awful because of road construction. Products and services are vulnerable to competition, commoditization. Technology can be antiquated. Every single thing most business owners think of as solid assets are actually paper-thin.

The only asset that can be kept safe from every threat and made to appreciate in value year after year is the relationship you have with your customers. Not just a list of customers. *Relationship* with customers.

Most business owners do a terrible, terrible, terrible job managing this asset. They take it for granted. They refuse to invest in it. They abuse it by communicating with it only when asking it for money.

Customer relationship depends on a number of factors. An important one is frequency of communication. A customer (or prospect) list loses about 10% of its value every month it is neglected. In 11 months, it's worth less than random names pulled from the white pages. Communication needs to be as frequent as it is welcomed and should be interesting, informative, entertaining, and personal as well as commercial. In my businesses, my best customers hear from us through a variety of means and media 232 times a year, not including overt promotions and offers. The minimum I set for my clients is 52, once a week. Most businesses' number is zero to a few. A few might as well be zero. You cannot sustain a relationship with an occasional, random drive-by and kiss thrown from the window of your car.

Another factor is consistency. Some aspect of your relationship ought to be ritualized and dependable. Like maintaining a relationship with the relative who lives a long distance away with the phone call every Saturday morning. The media devices we use most often for this are consistently published customer or member newsletters, customer birthday, anniversary, and seasonal greetings, and periodic events. These are appropriate for every business and every sales professional, and the most profitable businesses with the highest customer values in more than 256 different categories I have direct interaction with use them.

Another factor is quality of communication, creativity, and personality. In my book *The Ultimate Marketing Plan*, I make my case for the Ultimate Marketing Sin: being boring.

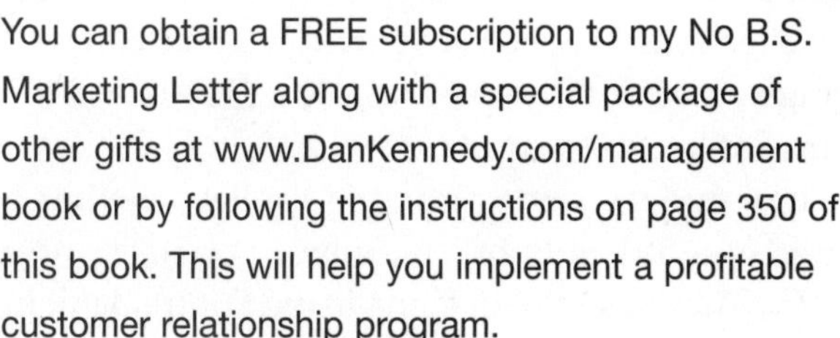

Recommended Resource #10

You can obtain a FREE subscription to my No B.S. Marketing Letter along with a special package of other gifts at www.DanKennedy.com/management book or by following the instructions on page 350 of this book. This will help you implement a profitable customer relationship program.

Customer Relationships as Equity

For every business, there is a Present Bank and a Future Bank. Both require attentive management.

The Present Bank has to do with today's sales and profits. At a restaurant, the Present Bank statistics to manage might include the number of tables turned per shift or the number of extra desserts or fine wines sold. Those will immediately affect the sales and profits deposited that day. The Future Bank has to do with customer relationships initiated or nurtured. Statistics to manage might include the number of Birthday Club Cards completed by customers or the number of customers who join the VIP Club. These have Future Bank Value. The thing to wrap your head around, although few business owners ever do, is that managing the Future Bank is as important as or more important than managing the Present Bank, because the Present Bank is merely income, and the Future Bank is equity. You can't, for example, sell me the income you've already spent. But you can sell me the *facts* that you have 2,300 people in your Birthday Club who will all, obviously, be having a birthday sometime in the next 12 months and again within 24 months and again within 36 months, and historically you get 70% of these Club Members to come in for their free dinner and bring three people with them, producing average checks of $100.00 . . . so there's 2,300 x 70% = 1,610 x 3-year average customer life span = 4,830 x $100.00 = $483,000.00 in the Future Bank. That's equity.

Believe it or not, the same principle applies whether you're a manufacturer of spud nuts or an equine podiatrist or a zebra stripe remover. There's a way to manage the Future Bank in nearly every business. You need to figure it out in yours.

The next chapter deals with other numbers you need to manage by.

Let me conclude here by saying that I think you ought to get rich. As rich as your business can possibly allow under the very best of created circumstances. Nothing less should be acceptable. It is my experience that just about any business, even small businesses, have the potential to make their owners quite rich—and a lot richer than those owners think. But it doesn't happen by accident. It requires very smart marketing and very tough-minded management. That's the work that's necessary for a business owner, service provider, or self-employed professional to move from just making a good living to creating real wealth.

I think we'd have a better society if all the rich people really knew and experienced how poor people live and all the poor people knew and understood how hard the rich people work.

OUR MOST IMPORTANT ASSET

Vincent Palko
www.AdToons.com

CHAPTER 43

Management by the Numbers (The Right Numbers)

Paying attention to numbers is a dull, tiresome routine, a drudgery. The more you want to know about your business, the more numbers there will be. They cannot be skimmed. They must be read, understood, thought about and compared with other sets of numbers which you have read that day, that week, or earlier that year.

—HAROLD GENEEN, FORMER PRESIDENT OF ITT, AND AUTHOR OF *MANAGING*

How can you govern a country which produces 246 different kinds of cheese?

—CHARLES DEGAULLE

I'll begin by saying that I personally hate everything that has to do with mathematics except counting money. If you do, too, I understand. I would also much rather be involved in creative activity than number crunching. If you are like that, too, I understand. However, we have to be mature enough not to let our want-tos totally control us.

The fact is, in 30 years, working with well over 1,000 clients, I've found that those who've made the most money and gotten wealthiest are the ones who know their numbers inside out, upside down, backward and forward, minute by minute, day by day.

When I meet with most business owners, I can stump them with the first three numbers questions I ask.

Most business owners also spend a lot of time looking at useless numbers. Most accountants give you history books and banker's numbers that are of little value in making good day-to-day decisions or even in accurately understanding what's going on in your business. The income statements and balance sheets prepared for the bankers and tax authorities reflect neither real income nor real worth.

Here are some of the most important numbers you need to monitor and manage in your business:

CPL
CPS
ATV
CV'S
LCV
CTP
PB
FB
EC/PC
QC
SE

And for yourself:

WA
EIEND

CPL = Cost per Lead
CPS = Cost per Sale
ATV = Average Transaction Value
CVs = Customer Values
LCV = Lifetime or Long-Term Customer Value
CTP = Contribution to Profit
PB = Present Bank
FB = Future Bank

EC/PC = Expense Creep/Problem Creep
QC = Quality Control
SE = Sales Effectiveness

And for yourself:

WA = Wealth Accumulation
EIEND = Enough Is Enough Number Deficit

As you might instantly guess, an entire book could be written just about this. In these few pages, I'll do my best to explain each category of statistics and why they're important.

Let's start with ATV, CVs, and LCV.

ATV, Average Transaction Value, has several uses. Average FIRST Transaction Value gives you a big-thumb number of which you may be willing to spend part, all, or 110%, 150%, or more to acquire a customer—and determining the maximum allowable cost of acquisition needs to be done before ever spending a dime on advertising and marketing. Beyond that, ATV as a continual measurement gives you a blink-of-an-eye look at how well or how poorly your selection of customers, your sales process, and your salespeople are doing overall, against same time prior year, and during special promotions. Increasing ATV is one of the few ways a mature business or a business at or near 100% capacity can actually increase income. And small ATV increases can equate to large net profit increases; if all fixed expenses are covered by, say, a $100.00 ATV and you can bump ATV by just $10.00 or 10%, the only deduction is cost of goods at, say, 50%, leaving $5.00. If the regular $100.00 loses not only cost of goods but another 30% to overhead and fixed expenses, you only net $20.00 from the regular or old $100.00 ATV. The little $10.00 bump to

ATV at the top gives you $5.00, a 25% increase in net. The constant "what can we do to increase ATV?" question is important. So is measuring and monitoring ATV.

CV, Customer Value, takes into consideration multiple transactions and buying behavior over a period of time. You need a way to monitor your average customer value within a prescribed time period, so you can segment your list into A-, B-, and C-level customers, to invest in them and communicate with them differently. This can also help you choose media, methods, and sources of customers better, by watching where A customers come from and where C customers come from; if there's a difference, up the use of the things attracting A's and drop the things attracting C's. Sometimes even field salespeople differ in the value of the customers they bring in; the one bringing in A's and B's should be kept, while the one bringing in mostly C's and a few B's has to go.

Then, CTP, Contribution to Profit, delves even deeper. It takes into consideration what customers buy and even how they behave. In most businesses, different products and services are more profitable than others, so naturally different customers are more profitable than others. And different customers spending the same amounts on the same products and services require different amounts of care. A big long-distance carrier made news and public controversy in mid-2007 by "firing" thousands of its "worst" (least profitable) customers, based on their excessive need for human customer service. Its average customer used a couple hours of customer service a month while these undesirable customers used 10, 20, even 30 hours. So the company sent them letters of termination and sent them elsewhere. The public and media outcry was: How dare it deprive these people of phone service? The smart shareholders' thought was: Finally. If you aren't measuring CTP, you are undoubtedly servicing customers who are actually costing you money to keep.

LCV, Lifetime Customer Value, needs to bundle CV and CTP, consider the length of time you keep customers active, and provide a number measuring the total value of a customer. This ultimately controls your decisions about how much to invest in obtaining your customers. It's also the number you deposit in your Future Bank the day you secure a new customer—or, possibly, re-activate a lost one. Knowing this number also helps keep you real about the costs of losing customers and helps you determine what you are willing to invest in keeping them.

Specific to managing your marketing and sales, there are three important numbers. When consulting with a client, I need to know and be able to manipulate CPL and CPS, Cost per Lead and Cost per Sale.

CPL is the money spent to get a prospect to raise his hand, step forward, and start down the path we've constructed for him. So, if you pay $1,000.00 a month for your Yellow Pages ad and it gets ten people a month to call or go to your web site, you have a CPL of $100.00 from that medium. CPL differs by medium but can also be greatly affected by what I work on most—the advertising and marketing message itself. CPL can be deceptive, as the source with the highest CPL may provide the lowest CPS. So this is a predictive but not definitive stat to watch and manage. **CPS is the truly critical number, because it reflects all the costs of putting the prospect on the path, moving him along the path, and ultimately converting him to a customer, client, or patient**. CPS will also vary by source, method, and the effectiveness of the path itself. From the previously described numbers, you have an MA-CPS, a Maximum Allowable CPS, and you work to get as many ways of bringing in customers as possible to perform at or below that number. I should tell you, hardly any business owner knows these numbers, although quite a few think they do. When somebody starts digging in, investigating, analyzing, and monitoring these numbers, they are usually amazed at how little they knew about what was really going on in their business.

I often get questions asked of me that can't be answered intelligently without these numbers. For example: "My Yellow Pages ad works pretty good. The rep is urging me to increase from a quarter page to a half page. Should I?" My questions then have to do with what "pretty good" really is:

1. What is the CPL from the ad?
2. What is the CPS from the ad?
3. What is the LCV of the customers obtained from the ad?
4. How do these values compare with the CPL, CPS, and LCV from all the other means you use to get customers?

And that's just the beginning, but if you can't at least answer those, I can't tell you whether to increase that ad's size, shrink it, eliminate it altogether, or, heck, buy two full pages!

And if you're buying ad media and investing in marketing without tracking these numbers, you aren't *managing* your business at all. You are *guessing* your business.

The other number related to this is SE, Sales Effectiveness. It's not really *a* number, but a collection of numbers. For example, the number of people who call in and are converted to kept appointments is an SE number, and its movement up or down will dramatically affect CPS. Also, the number of visitors to a web site induced to provide their full contact information and invite follow-up vs. those providing only an e-mail address vs. those providing no information at all is an SE issue. Of course, the biggest SE number is what happens when the prospect comes to your store, office, or showroom or invites you or your sales representative into his home or office and a sales presentation occurs. Here, the closing percentage and the size of the transaction combine to SE. Tolerating subpar performance with either number backs up through the entire system, making your CPS and CPL too high from some or all sources. Improving performance in either or both closing percentage and transaction size allows for higher CPL, providing competitive advantage in marketing, and provides better profits as well.

SE applies, incidentally, not just to situations where a salesman designated as a salesman is making a formal sales presentation to a prospect. It's broader. In a retail store in the mall, the number of people who walk in vs. the number who leave empty-handed after just browsing vs. the number who buy is an important SE statistic. So via recording every "ding" of a person walking across the threshold or from surveillance cameras, you have to know how many people walked in today. Then you look at how many different customer transactions there were. If 100 people walked in and you have 20 different purchases, you have, to be sloppy, a 20% SE number. With that in hand, you can begin working on merchandise, display, signage, offers, and staff—Sales Design® and Sales Choreography®—to improve the 20%. Without knowing it and monitoring it, you can't do anything about it. You would also measure ATV in that same store as another SE number.

Next, there are two numbers related to managing operations rather than managing marketing: EC/PC and QC. EC/PC stands for Expense Creep and Problem Creep. If freight was 8% of your gross in the first quarter of 2007 but is 11% for same quarter in 2008, it bears investigation. EC happens many ways. Vendors can inch prices up without being questioned, comparison shopped, or negotiated with. Theft can start occurring or increase. (I have a client who's freight bill went up nicely when his shipping clerk was shipping quite a bit of goods she was selling on eBay through his UPS and FedEx accounts. To add insult to injury, she was stealing the merchandise from him, too.) EC alarm bells should trigger investigation. PC is even more interesting. It's a way to try to quantify your mostly hidden "people costs" with employees, vendors, and customers alike. For example, let's say a vendor is late on promised deliveries 1 out of 20 times. But over time, it's 1 out of 16, 1 out of 12. Unchecked it'll be 1 for 1. The sooner stopped or the sooner the vendor gets replaced, the better. I have a big rule about all this you may have seen in my other books or heard me discuss: if I wake up three mornings in a row thinking about you and we aren't at least occasionally having sex, you gotta go. But managing relationships by PC can usually rid you of such problems before they reach the three-mornings-in-a-row stage.

QC, Quality Control, is again about translating vague ideas about how you're doing into quantifiable data about how well you're doing. There are a lot of tools to measure QC. Customer questionnaires and surveys, "How are we doing?" calls to a certain number of randomly selected customers each week, close monitoring of customers gone inactive and direct contact with them, mystery shopping, surveillance systems. QC is about compliance with your Program as well as customer perceptions and feedback. It's easier in manufacturing than in sales or service businesses. In manufacturing, you can, for example, randomly pull and check x number of items from each job or each shift, rate them on set criteria, and numerically grade the quality for the job, shift, day. You can monitor returns of merchandise for refunds due to defects. In nonmanufacturing environments, you have to work harder to assemble meaningful statistics.

A quick, amusing QC story. I had a very bad day in an upscale chain hotel, in Boston. I rather angrily filled out the full-page satisfaction guarantee with a thick, bold black marker and continued my comments on its back. I vented. In the morning, I forgot to take it downstairs and instead left it lying on the top of the desk in the room, with piles of other papers. When I returned that afternoon, it and only it had been removed by the maid. Gee, do you think she turned it in for me?

Finally, there are four money numbers I suggest managing carefully. PB and FB, Present Bank and Future Bank, have to do with income and equity. Most business owners focus entirely on the first and ignore the second. Simply put, you not only need a set of numbers you watch every day relevant to your business, reflective and predictive of income, but also need a set means of evaluating whether you've increased the value of the business today or not. I've discussed this earlier in the book.

Finally, WA and EIEND. WA, Wealth Accumulation, is the first number that actually gets to your primary responsibility as a business owner and primary purpose for business ownership (unless you very consciously and deliberately decide otherwise, as in *This little antique shop is really my hobby, and I don't care about the financial results*). If you are in business for business reasons, then **your <u>personal</u> WA is really what it's all about**. This means you have to be measuring your success by the amount of money you are able to take out of the business and put somewhere smart and safe, ideally in appreciating or income-generating assets. You should have preset goals for WA and be very, very grumpy if not meeting them and ruthless about making whatever changes are required to meet them. There's also a discipline for this, usually called "pay yourself first."

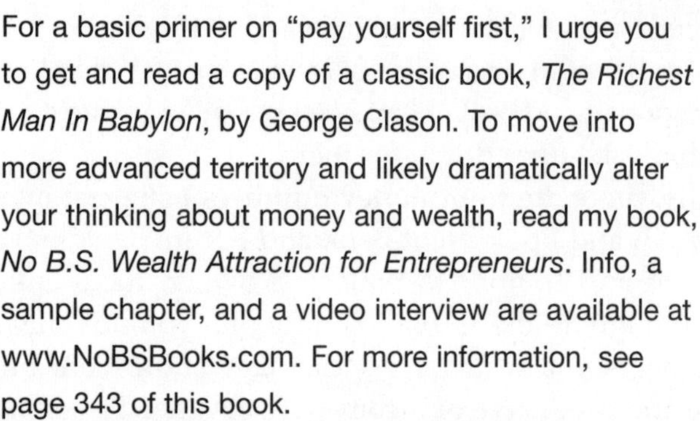

Recommended Resource #11

For a basic primer on "pay yourself first," I urge you to get and read a copy of a classic book, *The Richest Man In Babylon*, by George Clason. To move into more advanced territory and likely dramatically alter your thinking about money and wealth, read my book, *No B.S. Wealth Attraction for Entrepreneurs*. Info, a sample chapter, and a video interview are available at www.NoBSBooks.com. For more information, see page 343 of this book.

EIEND is a very interesting measurement hardly anybody uses but me. Years back, I determined what my Enough-Is-Enough Number was. The EIEN is that sum of money you have invested in income-producing "untouchables" that will allow you to never need to earn another dollar as long as you live. Your EIEN has to take into consideration whether you want to leave a certain size estate to your heirs or are happy on the "die broke plan," eventually eating all the principal, ideally with your very last check bouncing as they close the lid . . . exactly how much you want to spend every month . . . reserves for health care . . . and other factors. It is admittedly an imprecise number, because of semi-unpredictable matters like inflation, divorce, suddenly deciding at age 80 you want to take up hot air balloon racing. But a well-considered number is a lot better than no number at all. And you may reset the number if you get close more quickly than expected, although constantly pushing the number higher defeats its purpose. Anyway, once establishing this number, I kept it on every page of my checkbook and deducted from it the amounts of money moved out of my business into my personal WA accounts and investments. Every day, or at least every time I used the company checkbook, I saw the EIEND, the Deficit, the gap between where I was and where I aspired to be, and the shrinkage of that gap (or lack thereof). This motivated me in many ways, but most importantly to move money out of my business to my personal WA.

To offer full disclosure, I went nearly the first two of three decades of my prime business years without EIEND monitoring or effective use of many of these other numbers. As a result, I was a high-income, underinvested guy. I think I made some very poor decisions as a result. Literally the minute I started evaluating myself in this way, I rapidly got better at investing, and I dramatically accelerated my personal wealth accumulation. I went way past my original EIEN several years ago, and again went several years without such measurement, only to recently reinstate it, and again immediately recognize positive changes in my decision making, my personal motivation, and my wealth accumulation.

As I said, I hate math. But I've learned to be very, very interested in this kind of "money math." And as I said, business owners who aren't, aren't really *managing* their businesses. They are *guessing* their businesses.

CHAPTER 44

How to Profit from the Age of Tolerated Mass Incompetence and the Coming Monster Recession

Following a nuclear attack on the United States, the United States Postal Service plans to distribute Emergency Change of Address Cards.

—U.S. FEDERAL EMERGENCY MANAGEMENT (FEMA) EXECUTIVE ORDER #11490

When I was in my teens, I came across a book I've since lost and can no longer remember the exact title or author of, but its title was something like *How to Profit from the Coming Crash*. I read it and was fascinated. It was the first time it was made clear to me that there was such a thing as "crisis investing," that one man's crash was another man's boom, and that you could, in fact, profit from circumstances everybody around you viewed as "awful." One of the chapters in the book profiled people who got rich during the Great Depression begun in 1929, some by buying real estate and hotels and businesses, some by starting particular types of businesses. In history classes

I was shown a Great Depression that encompassed all of America and everyone in it; pictures of shoeless people in camps eating beans from cans; desolation, destruction, and despair. But in this book I was presented with a different picture of that same time—a picture of ambitious, optimistic investors and entrepreneurs eagerly embracing a whole new array of opportunities to get rich. This came in handy later when Jimmy Carter got elected and single-handedly created the second great depression. (Many readers will be too young to recall this and have no frame of reference. Summary: double-digit interest rates, double-digit inflation, double-digit unemployment, and mile-long gas lines to boot.) By then I knew that there is no such thing as a "good" economy or "bad" economy for the person agile of mind and action, who creates his own economy.

NO B.S. Ruthless Management Truth #9

To paraphrase Napoleon Hill, in every crisis lies the seeds of one or more equal or greater opportunities. The person agile of mind and action can create his own economy.

Crisis Opportunity

"Crisis opportunity" actually comes around frequently and repeatedly in different sectors of business and economy.

Recessions of a sort limited to a single segment of the business world and public economy. For example, as I was putting the finishing touches on this book, we were in the early stage of a potential tidal wave of residential real estate foreclosures and forfeitures, flooding banks and lenders with a predicted 1.2 million to 1.6 million properties in an 18-month period. That's more than 65,000 a month. Over 2,000 every day. A crisis if you own, manage, or own stock in a lending institution that has been aggressive and "loose" with its lending standards. The opportunity of a lifetime if you know how to buy foreclosures, how to "flip" and sell or rent properties, have some capital and time. If you do, you can buy dollar bills for 40 to 60 cents each.

It is my belief there is a "crisis opportunity" rapidly developing and likely to explode in the very near future that will destroy many businesses and destroy the profit margins of many others, but present an incredible opportunity to a relatively small number of businesses in each category who ready themselves to profit.

The "crisis opportunity" has two parts, converging at a meeting point visible on the horizon.

One is an utter and complete collapse of even minimally acceptable service and basic competence. You can see it coming. Wherever possible, businesses are replacing and will continue to replace incompetent, unreliable, expensive humans with automation. That was once restricted to the factory, but it is now part of the ironically titled customer service environment. The Industrial Revolution is long over, but the service revolution has just begun. Automation is replacing service people just as it did factory workers. Beyond that, consumers are forced into pumping their own gas, banking at ATMs and online rather than face-to-face with a teller, even ordering pizza online by doing their own data entry. In each application, it began or is beginning as a choice for consumers. In every application the goal is to make it the only choice. Wherever possible, other customer service jobs are being outsourced overseas to cheaper labor. Every place from the retail store to the casino floor has fewer and fewer service people, more and more do-it-yourself options, longer waits, poorer service. This will kill some businesses. But, for all businesses who participate in this trend, it will fully and completely commoditize them, end all consumer preference, and liberate consumers to go wherever the cheapest price is offered. There will be nothing to influence buying but price. That, of course, shrinks margins to the bone and further thins the herd.

The second is an overall, broad, across-economic-segments recession. You can see it coming, too. Too much of the most recent boom has been based on "irrational exuberance" (to quote Greenspan) and ridiculously profligate spending, drunken-sailor use of consumer credit, conversion of all home equity into depreciating assets like boats and vacations and Taj Mahal kitchen remodeling. All made possible by nonsensically suppressed interest rates and the impact of President Bush's tax cuts. This produced a remarkably resilient economy, able to thrive even under the burden of an incredibly expensive war. But if ever there was an overinflated balloon just waiting to burst, this is it. Add much pressure, say, from a liberal President and Congress eager to tax the pants off "the rich," lay on a bank-breaking socialist health-care system, make "free" preschool and college available to all; or from finally rising interest rates and stagnating or dropping real estate values; or from stock market correction backward by 1,000 or 2,000 points or more possibly, partly spurred by liberals' announced desire to raise capital gains taxes to equal income taxes; or—well, the list goes on. Any of many ignition switches will do. Then we'll see Jimmy Carter Part 2 or worse. In many ways it's an enema the country badly needs. But it's gonna hurt.

So, when these two freight trains collide head-on, as I fear they will, will it be possible not only to survive but actually to thrive in business? Yes, you can prosper to a greater degree than ever before. There are only two key things you need to do. First, provide an ever escalating, exceptional, even phenomenal level of customer service, delivered by exceptionally competent, highly trained, highly incentivized, and well-policed humans. Go in the opposite direction of the masses of businesses in your field and in general. As they cut back on service, as they increasingly disappoint consumers and sanction incompetence from their employees, you be the one to increase, expand, and improve service, to invest more in providing service and in employees who perform. Second, design your business and aim your marketing at the affluent consumers who are least affected by overall

Recommended Resource #12

My *No B.S. Marketing to the Affluent/Mass Affluent Letter* is totally devoted to news, insight, strategies and examples of successfully marketing to the affluent and redesigning businesses to do so. Information is available at www.DanKennedy.com.

economy ups and downs, who do not use price as a decision factor, who have a demonstrated preference for exceptional service and a willingness to pay for it.

In short, the business pyramid is going to change in shape, to something with a starving, struggling, barely surviving crowd of commoditized businesses delivering little or no service and selling at minimum margins at the bottom, no middle, and at a peak, very different businesses selling at premium prices and enjoying higher than ever margins by delivering extraordinary service to affluent customers. Right now there's a big middle—think moving from Wal-Mart to Target to Kohl's to J.C. Penney to Dillard's and Macy's to Nordstrom and Neiman Marcus. The middle will disappear. Not permanently, of course, but long enough to do serious damage. (See Figure 44.1.)

The difference determining whether you fall to the bottom or rise to the top will not be in products or brand names or physical location or any factor other than the existence or nonexistence, extent, and quality of your customer service. If you follow the crowd on its current path of shrinking service, sanctioning incompetence, and merely trying not to be worse than others in your category, you'll follow the crowd off the cliff. If you turn your back on the crowd and head in the exact opposite direction, you'll soon arrive at the land of milk 'n' honey.

The only other option is to devise a business requiring few or zero people involved in any way other than yourself but that cannot be automated and commoditized. This applies, for example, to very high-priced professionals providing a service. If this is you, then you may have the opportunity to shrink your business's size and get rid of all employees, raise your fees even more, and deal with a small, select number of clients.

"Concierge" medical and dental practices represent a small, current, controversial trend that moves doctors in this direction. But failing this, if you are going to compete in the big marketplace, all your middle options will disappear, and you will choose to either (1) "bottom feed," providing minimalist service and rock-bottom prices in a place where extinction always looms as there's always some big, dumb, unprofitable but well-capitalized company or some small business fool willing to sell cheaper or (2) step way up to the tiny peak of the pyramid, providing truly extraordinary service to a small segment of the market. Better to choose now than wait until you must do so under crisis circumstances.

Incidentally, this movement can be seen in certain industries and companies already. Disney has started promoting a new "personal guide service" at its parks, at $125.00 an hour—and I predict that price doubling and consumers eagerly paying it in very short order. It's only one of many examples of Disney creating new "for the affluent" options in goods, services, and at its resorts and parks. Luxury hotels are adding ultraluxury suites with personal chefs and butlers. And hotels are adding upscale hotels inside themselves, such as the Four Seasons inside Mandalay Bay in Las Vegas. The boom in "marketing to the affluent" that I began focusing my newsletter subscribers and clients on beginning in 2005 is actually a precursor to the entire disappearance of the middle of the pyramid, a movement of forward-thinking companies and entrepreneurs to the top of the new pyramid.

Last, I'd be remiss if I didn't mention the related antiproductivity, antiwork crisis developing. A piece on the *Today Show* that I saw as I was completing this book was titled "Friday Is the New

Saturday." It revealed the quiet surrender of hundreds of big U.S. corporations to a 4½ day workweek, inviting people to come in only one hour early on Friday mornings, then leave at noon because "nobody does any work Friday afternoons." Employees spend Friday afternoons planning their weekends, thinking about their weekends, calling and texting and e-mailing people about their weekends, so these employers have acquiesced and written off those Friday afternoons. Fools—now nobody will do any work Friday mornings. And when all of Friday is surrendered, Thursday afternoon will be the new Friday afternoon. Where does it end? Probably where Outback Steakhouse's® TV ads were the day I completed this book: they have proclaimed Wednesday as the new Friday. An entire generation of workers is making it abundantly clear they do not value work, do not equate work to honor, have no work ethic, and have very little interest in work. Their jobs are evil inconveniences. Our society is becoming French, all about leisure and lifestyle. As I was finishing this, obviously months before you are reading it, the hottest "business" (I use the term loosely) book was Tim Ferriss's *The 4-Hour Work Week*. Personally, I like Tim, and Tim writes about me as having great influence on him, which I appreciate. But frankly, the fact that this title resonated with so many people that it made the book a huge bestseller, and that so many people never questioned the plausibility of its premise, does not bode well for anybody trying to get 40 hours of honest productivity out of people. The warning signs are all around you. While it is difficult to get productivity from people now, that's only going to get a whole lot worse before it gets better, if it ever does.

The only way to turn *that* to your advantage is to design a business that needs fewer employees and can pay them overly generously, so that you can attract and keep the absolute cream of the crop, so that you can deliver the truly extraordinary service that will keep you at the peak of the new pyramid. And you will need every trick in this book to make that work!

FIGURE 44.1

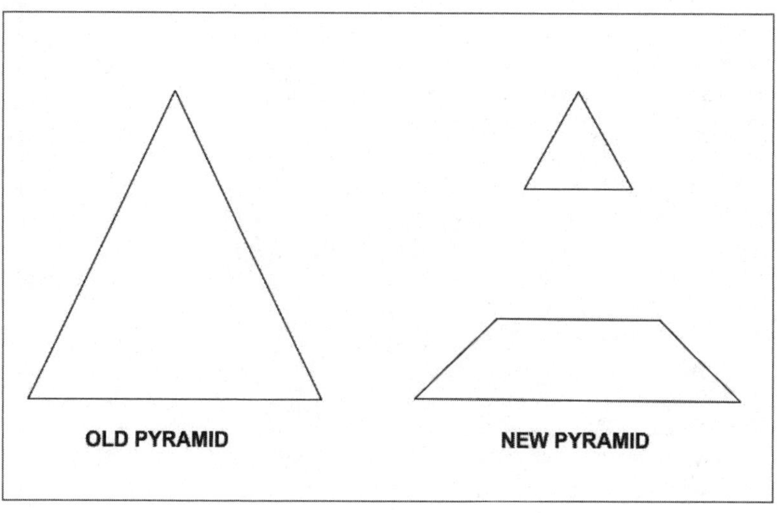

CHAPTER 45

In the Next 12 Months

In my first 12 months we marketed 107 new product initiatives across 22 countries. Every existing product was repackaged and most were reconceived, reformulated or relaunched.

—ALBERT DUNLAP, TURNAROUND WIZARD AND AUTHOR OF *MEAN BUSINESS: HOW I SAVE BAD COMPANIES AND MAKE GOOD COMPANIES GREAT*

If you have read this far, congratulations. Most people who buy business books never actually read them! But the next step is action. The real question is: What will you DO—what will you get DONE—as a result of your thinking spurred by having read this book?

My friend, speaking colleague, and author Jim Rohn says, "Poor people have big TVs. Rich people have big libraries." That's true as far as it goes. But the entrepreneurs I know and hang out with who develop amazing businesses and create exceptional wealth can, as I can, walk you through their big libraries and tell you what actions they took as a result of each of the hundreds and hundreds of books on the shelves.

And I would pose an even tougher question to you: What will get DONE in the next 12 months?

Foolish people try to escape pressure. Successful people deliberately put themselves under pressure to perform. Extremely successful people put themselves under extreme pressure to perform—and thrive on it.

I frequently work with entrepreneurs on triggering what we call The Phenomenon—a time when you accomplish more in 12 months than in the previous 12 years. That's possible. It happens a lot. It happens to just about every ambitious, hardworking entrepreneur at some time in his life. But it can be *made to happen* immediately. One of the most powerful triggers is the *deciding*. Determining everything you will get DONE in the next 12 months, the next 12 weeks, the next 12 days, the next 12 hours, even the next 12 minutes, then racing the calendar and the clock, declaring war on the resistance, opposition, and sluggishness of those around you, and placing yourself and others under extreme pressure to perform. (Those who crack under the pressure need to be discarded and replaced.) So I urge you not to put this book away on a shelf or loan it to a friend until you first bolt

Recommended Resource #13

Visit www.InTheNext12Months.com/books for exciting information about "The Phenomenon" and how you can turn it on for yourself, in your business life!

yourself in a room with nothing but it, a legal pad, a pen, and caffeine and go through it again page by page, and think, and decide what you will get DONE in your business in the next 12 months, 12 weeks, 12 days. Your lists may include things you've been tolerating that you will no longer tolerate, people who should have been replaced already who now will be, new initiatives in marketing, sales, training, and supervision, reshuffling of priorities and people, and more.

Don't just read the book. Make the lists. DO. Get DONE. Fast. Ruthlessly when need be.

CHAPTER 46

Nine Steps to Optimizing Your Business Exit

BY HARVEY ZEMMEL

Over the years, you've invested money, time, blood, sweat, and tears into your business. While you may have enjoyed a good income during those years, most business owners look to their exit as a time of cashing in on accumulated equity. Or, you may have sacrificed income in order to re-invest in your business. Either way, optimizing the financial gain from your exit is important, but too often assumed.

Fact: more than 75% of all businesses put up for sale NEVER sell. Worse, the majority of business owners who do sell are shocked, disappointed, and unhappy with the price they get. If you want to have a different, successful exit experience, there are nine basic steps to follow.

Step 1: Begin with the End in Mind

Whether you are planning on selling your business ten months or ten years from now, you should be working on it now. You need to consider an array of important questions and develop goals from them, for example: What price range do you want to sell for? Do you want to stay attached to the business in some way? For what length of time? Or do you want to completely and immediately retire? What do you want for staff, family, and associates who may be involved with or dependent on your business?

You also need to develop scenarios for possible sale. This means determining well in advance, by category or by name, who the likely buyers of the business may be, so you can think about why they will buy, what will be attractive to them, and how you might need to adapt your business in advance to fit their preferences. **It's not enough to create value. It is important to create *saleable* value,** and to do that you have to consider the potential buyers' means of calculating value. Incidentally the majority of business that sell for top dollar sell to unobvious types of buyers, so creative thought in considering all possible buyers is important.

With a vision of what your business needs to look like, act like, and perform like when you finally engineer your exit, you can move toward that target.

Step 2: Create Value, Not Just Income or Profit

You do <u>not</u> want your business's marketability and selling price to be defined by a simple multiple of earnings or cash flow. Instead, you want to create higher value from a complex set of factors, including demonstrated but not fully exploited potential value. To create value in a business rather than just income, you may have to assume the role of Chief Value Creator, not Worker. Are you building yourself a valuable, saleable business or just a glorified job?

Over a term of just eight years, I built one of my businesses from scratch to a value of more than $30 million. That means, on average, every day I worked, I added $10,273.00 of real, saleable value to my business. Then, I was still developing my system for building value, with what I know and use with clients today, I could have done it in half the time. To add that kind of value every day, you just can't afford to be working in your business like an employee. This forces you to change the way you use and invest your time and to be ruthless in managing your time.

Step 3: Build Your Exit Plan NOW

There are a lot of options and opportunities for exit, not just an outright sale for a huge cash payout. You might want your company to go public and extract your cash through stock and stock options. You might want to delay your exit but sell part or all of your business to a much larger company and stay on it as its CEO, able to expand and achieve bigger goals with the parent's more substantial resources and synergies at your disposal. You might want family to take over the business. These options involve plans for a staged exit over years, rather than all at one time. While flexibility is required, it's important to create plans in advance, so you begin shaping the business accordingly.

This kind of planning will help you break out of the "glorified employee" mentality and motivate development of better systems, better people, better delegation, so your business's day-to-day operations are less and less dependent on you and readily assumable by a buyer, and you are freed up to think and act more like an investor creating value.

Step 4: Focus on "Key Metrics" of Your Business

When a knowledgeable buyer is considering your business, the first thing he'll look for are key statistics that give a shorthand answer or quick snapshot to how well your business is doing, how much it might be worth, and how attractive it might be to acquire. In every industry, these key statistics, or "metrics," are different and unique. There are industry norms and averages for these metrics, so your business can be compared, favorably or unfavorably, with other business in your category.

In the industry in which I built the $30 million company (aged care facilities), the key metrics had to do with occupancy levels and net profits. Occupancy levels were predictive, profits historical. Because I made the statistics in these categories just a few percentage points higher than the average business in the industry, my company was valued at about twice the average value. Marginal superiority equaled disproportionately multiplied value. The same principle is true in every industry. If your key metrics exceed industry norms by even a little, your business can have a much higher selling price.

Again, every type of business has its own unique metrics. If you have a retail business, they include gross sales, net profits, turnover of inventory, return on dollars put into inventory, customer value, and others. If you have a restaurant, there are different metrics. If it is a dental practice or small manufacturing company or a mail-order firm, each has its own metrics. You have to know what these are, know what your industry norms are, and use these to shape and manage your business. Most owners do not have a good "management by matrix of metrics" system in place, and when I help them develop and use one, they benefit in the short term with improved profits and in the long term with greater value created.

Step 5: Build Profits to Boost Selling Value

Profits aren't everything, and even unprofitable business get sold to buyers shopping for bargains and "fixer-uppers" or with different criteria of value. But generally speaking, profits will have a huge bearing on your business's valuation and selling price.

Increasing profits is rarely as simple as increasing sales. Increasing your database of customers, improving your communication with those clients, and improving their frequency of purchasing, the average size of their purchases, their overall retention, and overall value is all manageable. Also, your advertising, marketing, and use of both offline and online media affect profits as well as the attractiveness of the business. Creating multiple income streams, stable income, and above-average profits typically requires plugging a lot of holes and establishing more thorough procedures than a business owner mired in working in his business has.

Step 6: Timing the Sale of Your Business

Most owners sell their business because they decide to retire, they're going through a divorce, the family members they'd hoped would be interested in it aren't, they run up against ill health, or business is in a downturn. These are all negative situations that create time pressure and urgency and tend to harm the sale rice or terms. **If you want to get the maximum selling price and maximize your exit, you need as many conditions in your favor as possible.** This probably means selling when your industry is doing well or expected to do well in the future and your business has shown increasing profits over recent years. You need to time the sale of your business to optimize your exit, not for pure personal preference or convenience, and not under duress.

Step 7: Groom Your Business

When the time does come to sell, you need to polish things a bit. If you're selling a house, you trim the hedges, mow the lawns, clean the rooms. Common sense tells you to make your business look as attractive as possible to potential buyers. That may mean physical and cosmetic improvements to the place itself, including something as simple as a fresh coat of paint, or clearing away old inventory, as well as more complicated steps, like having all financial information in order and organized in a presentation format.

Step 8: Think Like a Buyer

Ask yourself questions like these: If I were thinking of buying this business, what would I want to know? What would I want to see? What might worry me? What information would motivate me to make an immediate buying decision? To pay a premium price?

Step 9: Negotiate the Best Possible Deal from a Position of Strength

Most business owners attempt negotiating with only one potential buyer, often a buyer who has come along at random; with poor timing, with poor preparation. You can negotiate from a position of strength only when you have brought several interested buyers forward at the same time who will feel urgency to outbid each other and when you have fully prepared to justify your desired price and terms. Developing knowledge about, and even relationships with, potential buyers well in advance of actually putting your business up for sale is one way of ensuring you will have more than one candidate when the time comes to pull the trigger. This will also empower you to walk away from a deal if it doesn't really suit your goals.

Maximizing your exit is a natural and integral part of managing your business, not something to be attended to only at the 11th hour.

HARVEY ZIMMEL is the world's leading authority on business exit strategies for small- to medium-sized businesses. He provides resources, training, mentoring, and coaching to business owners, entrepreneurs, and executives committed to getting the maximum price and desired outcome when they sell their businesses. For a FREE COPY of his special report *How to Avoid the 7 Most Common Mistakes You Can Make When Selling Your Business*, visit www.MaximizeYourExit.com.

CHAPTER 47

Your Support Circles

Help.
I need somebody!

—John Lennon and Paul McCartney, "Help!"

Owning, leading, and running a business can be a lonely business, and the isolation of entrepreneurship can have many negative consequences. While I personally appear to work alone to the casual observer, I have actually created "support circles" around me, and I believe you need to do the same.

We'll start closest to you and work out.

Circle 1 is your inner, inner, inner circle. Lee Iacocca talked and wrote about his "five horses," the people closest to him whom he trusted, was on the same page with, who understood him, who were qualified and able to offer worthwhile advice and ready and able to facilitate and implement his decisions. This inner, inner circle must be small to be valuable. It may (or may not) include your spouse, your business partner, and a "wise old man" mentor, and they may (or may not) be employees, paid advisors, or friends. You need to exercise enormous care about choosing the members of this team, as well as great vigilance toward their developing any agendas in conflict with your own.

Circle 2 is composed of experts, specialists, and providers of information. For many of my clients, this includes me. For me, there is one person above all others I rely on for information and advice about online marketing, another for the securing of celebrities for my clients' advertising campaigns, another for printing and publishing. And so forth. For me and probably you, this has to include at least one CPA, one or more other financial advisors, and one lawyer.

Either Circle 1 or Circle 2 needs to include the Man Who Makes You Defend Your Position. This is someone with considerable successful and relevant experience, no interest in mollifying or pleasing you, no agenda, little tact, and a great ability for asking tough and provocative questions. Someone willing to tell you he thinks you're making a huge mistake, with enough credibility you'll consider his position even though it displeases you. This is not the same as the buffoon who always has 100 reasons something can't be done but never has any ideas about how to accomplish anything. That's a minimum-wage loser. Here, I'm talking about high-value talent. Someone of real authority with whom you can argue your ideas, to improve them.

Circle 3 is made up of conduits and liaisons. For some of my clients, I'm on this list, too. These are people who know people you do not, who can refer you to reliable vendors you do not know, who can broker introductions for you with others. When I need to know something in the area of real estate, there are a few experts in my Circle 2 whom I can call on, and there are others in Circle 3 whom I can call on who can connect me to the right people. This circle should be as large as you can make it, your Rolodex® of useful and potentially useful contacts.

Circle 4 consists of high-performance, high-reliability vendors and suppliers. You'll have your own nuanced definitions of *high performance* and *high reliability*, but for me, these are providers of essential goods and services who perform with little or no supervision, who can think, who make promises they can keep and keep the promises they make as a matter of honor, not just because of a contract, and who practice the kind of management I've described in this book so they actually have the internal capability to do the job right the first time, on time. As an aside, you rarely get such vendors at the cheapest prices. I advise my clients to adjust the prices, margins, and economics of their businesses so they can afford paying premium prices and fees to top-notch vendors. If you surround yourself with the cheapest suppliers in this circle, you'd better stock up on Tums® and Tylenol®.

It is vital not to get lazy or complacent about maintaining the best possible Circles 2 and 4. Here, as with your employees, they all go lame. You must be demanding, critical, must measure performance and value, must be alert for slippage in attentiveness to you and performance, willing to fire, to churn 'n' burn without procrastination, and always searching for the next, better replacement.

Circle 5 is a "looser" group of mentors, consultants, coaches, peers, and colleagues, paid and unpaid; essentially, the people you select to associate with. Association is one of the most powerful factors influencing or sabotaging personal and professional success. Being deliberate about whom you do NOT associate with is as important as choosing whom you do associate with. "Lie down with dogs, wake up with fleas" is a ruthlessly truthful Japanese proverb. And it only takes one co-habitation to get infested with fleas. By "fleas," I mean negative and unproductive thoughts, limiting or erroneous beliefs, guilt, doubt, complacency, procrastination, weakened resolve, poverty thoughts, and so on. You need to associate exclusively with people who reinforce your personal motivation, encourage and celebrate your achievement, and are qualified through successful and relevant business or life experience to offer opinions and ideas worthy of your consideration. To be simplistic, and to paraphrase Trump, there are winners and there are losers. You win by hanging around winners. You lose by hanging around losers. No one you associate with leaves you untouched.

Recommended Resource #14

You can obtain a FREE GUEST PASS to a Glazer-Kennedy Insider's Circle™ local Chapter meeting, if there is a Chapter in your area, by accessing the Directory of Advisors/Chapters at www.DanKennedy.com. FREE two-months' membership with my newsletter and other benefits, see page 350.

With this in mind, I encourage entrepreneurs to participate in formal associations with other success-oriented entrepreneurs, and Glazer-Kennedy Insider's Circle™ provides such opportunities at both a local and an international level. We have local Chapters for our Members in more than 80 cities and areas throughout the United States and Canada, and local Kennedy Study Groups in many of those same areas, facilitated by our Certified No B.S. Advisors. We also have an international coaching and mastermind group facilitated only by phone, print media, and an online community; a higher international group, our Peak Performers Group, that meets for three two-day meetings a year led by Bill Glazer, CEO of Glazer-Kennedy Insider's Circle™ (author of Chapter 27) and Lee Milteer; and higher-level, small groups led by Bill and myself. These are, in a sense, "support groups" for like-minded entrepreneurs utilizing my advertising, marketing, sales, management, and wealth strategies. Other groups I recommend include the CEO Clubs founded by Joe Mancusco and groups in different niche industries and professions led by the experts I consult with and mentor. If you are unfamiliar with the "mastermind principle" at the foundation of all these groups, or should you opt to organize one of your own, I urge you to read both *Laws of Success* and *Think and Grow Rich,* by Napoleon Hill. You'll discover that these groups go back at least as far as the Industrial Revolution when, for example, Henry Ford, Thomas Edison, and Harvey Firestone deliberately formed their own "mastermind group." And you'll find the ingredients of a successful, productive group or a failed group clearly described.

Circle 6 is composed of living and dead authors from whom you seek, collect, and organize ideas, information, and sage advice. All business leaders are great readers. If you are not, you are at an extreme disadvantage. Books worth reading including

FIGURE 47.1: Support Circles

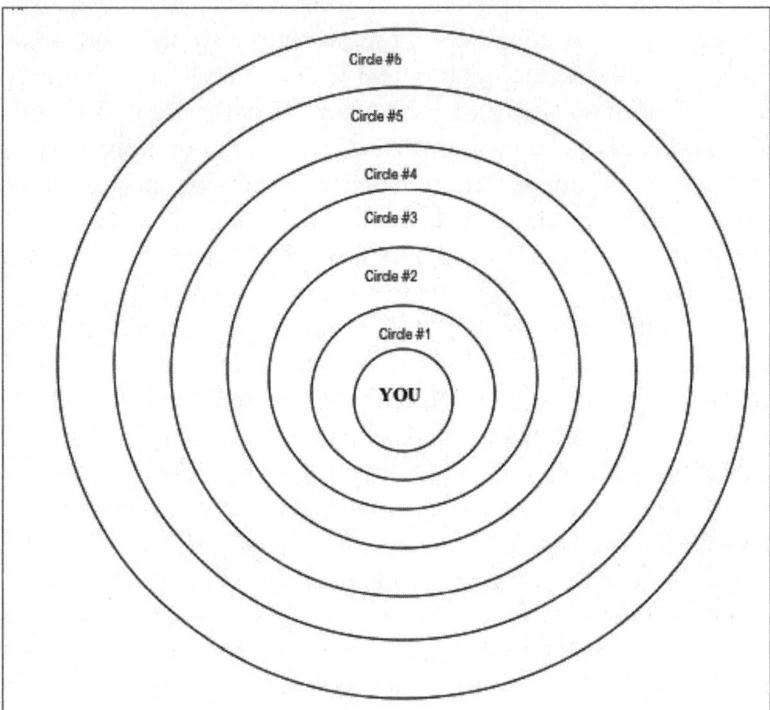

Circle #1: Inner, inner, inner circle

Circle #2: Experts, specialists, and providers of information

Circle #3: Liaisons and conduits

Circle #4: High-performance, high-reliability vendors and suppliers

Circle #5: "Looser" group of mentors, consultants, coaches, peers, and colleagues

Circle #6: Your Dialogue with the Dead

highly successful entrepreneurs' autobiographies and biographies about them (for example, Conrad Hilton's autobiography is free for the taking in the nightstand drawer of every Hilton hotel), legitimate experts' how-to books, and business opinion and strategy books like this one. I don't think you're "with it" if not reading at least one such book a week, and in my peak years, I read one a day. You should also develop a "top shelf" of books you reread once a year or more often, of key authors whose entire body of work you choose to get and keep and refer to frequently. In essence, an advisory board of authors accessed through their writings. You may even come to know a few so well you can ask yourself, "What would ______ do in this position?"—even carry on conversations with them in what Dr. Maltz called "the theater of your mind" (see the book *The New Psycho-Cybernetics*). In addition, there is a wealth of comparable material available in audio CDs, books on CD, seminars on CD, teleseminars, webinars, and current input from your chosen author-experts via their newsletters.

Carefully managing and using all six of these circles multiplies your personal power and enables you to get much more accomplished much faster than the typical business owner who establishes "rut-ines" and sticks with them almost entirely absent of input or outreach.

About the Author

DAN KENNEDY is a serial entrepreneur who has started, bought, built, and sold businesses of varied types and sizes. He is a highly sought after and outrageously well-paid direct-marketing consultant and direct-response copywriter, coach to groups of entrepreneurs, nearly retired professional speaker, author, equal opportunity annoyer, provocateur, and professional harness racing driver. He lives with his second and third wife (same woman) and a small dog in Ohio and Virginia. His office that he never visits is in Phoenix.

He welcomes your comments and can be reached directly only by fax at (602) 269-3113 or by mail at Kennedy Inner Circle, Inc., 5818 N. 7th Street #103, Phoenix, AZ 85014. (Do NOT e-mail him via any of the web sites presenting his information and publications. He does not use e-mail.)

He is occasionally available for interesting speaking engagements and very rarely accepts new consulting clients. Inquiries should be directed to the above office.

All information about his newsletters, how-to products, other resources, and Glazer-Kennedy Insider's Circle™ annual Marketing and Moneymaking SuperConferences and annual Info-Summit™ at which Dan appears, can be accessed online at www.DanKennedy.com, and by click-link, the online catalog and web store. A Directory of local Glazer-Kennedy Insider's Circle™ Chapters offering networking meetings, seminars, and Kennedy Study Groups in more than 80 cities can also be accessed at www.DanKennedy.com. If you enjoyed this book, you'll enjoy getting together with other business owners in your area applying Kennedy strategies! Other web sites of interest: www.RenegadeMillionaire.com and www.NoBSBooks.com. Dan's horse racing activities can be seen at www.NorthfieldPark.com.

Partial List of Authors, Business Leaders, Celebrities, etc. with Whom Dan Has Appeared on Programs with as a Speaker

Legendary Entrepreneurs
Donald Trump
Jim McCann, CEO, 1-800-Flowers*
Joe Sugarman, Blu-Blockers*
Debbi Fields, Founder, Mrs. Fields Cookies*
Mark McCormack, Founder, IMG Sports Management*

Authors and Speakers
Zig Ziglar*
Brian Tracy*
Jim Rohn*

Tom Hopkins*
Mark Victor Hansen (Chicken Soup for the Soul)*
Tony Robbins*

Political and World Leaders
Presidents Ford, Reagan, and Bush #1*
Gen. Norman Schwarzkopf*
Secretary Colin Powell*
Lady Margaret Thatcher*
Mikhail Gorbachev*

Broadcasters
Larry King*
Paul Harvey*

Hollywood Personalities
Bill Cosby*
Christopher Reeve*
Mary Tyler Moore*
Johnny Cash
The Smothers Brothers

Sports Personalities
George Foreman*
Joe Montana*
Peyton Manning*
Coaches Tom Landry*, Jimmy Johnson*, Lou Holtz*
Olympians Mary Lou Retton* and Bonnie Blair*

**Indicates repeated appearances on same platform.*

Other Books by Dan S. Kennedy

Titles in the No B.S. Series Published by Entrepreneur Press

No B.S. BUSINESS Success

21 Eternal Business Truths; How Entrepreneurs Really Make Big Money; How to Create Sales and Marketing Breakthroughs; Staying Sane in an Insane World

"Dan has written a book you can use immediately to get better, faster results . . . his approach is direct, his ideas are controversial, his ability to get results for his clients unchallenged. When you read learn and apply what you discover in these pages, your business life and your income will change forever."

—Brian Tracy

No B.S. SALES Success

33 Strategies; Positive Power of Negative Preparation; How to Stop Prospecting Once and for All; 6-Step Sales Process that (Almost) Never Fails; Takeaway Selling

"Dan has literally eliminated the B.S. in explaining great ways to make more sales."

—Tom Hopkins

No B.S. TIME MANAGEMENT for Entrepreneurs

9 Time Truths; Dan's Personal Strategies for Peak Productivity; The Care, Feeding, and Slaughter of Time Vampires; How to

Turn Time into Wealth; The Magic Power that Makes You Unstoppable; How to Accurately Value Your Time.

No B.S. DIRECT MARKETING for NON-Direct Marketing Businesses
(With Audio CD)
The 10 Rules; The Results Triangle; Making the Switch From Ineffective, Unaccountable Image/Brand and Big, Dumb Company Advertising/Marketing to Direct Response; Nine Comprehensive Case Histories Covering Every Type of Business; Putting an Iron Cage Around Your Customers

No B.S. WEALTH ATTRACTION for Entrepreneurs
(With "Live Seminar" Audio CD)
How to Stop Chasing Money and Let It Chase You; Overcoming Wealth Inhibition; Personal and Business Wealth Magnets; Converting Ordinary Businesses to Extraordinary Wealth Attraction Machines. (Based on Dan's Most Popular One-Day Seminar)

Coming Soon: *No B.S. MARKETING TO THE AFFLUENT*

FREE INFORMATION, SAMPLE CHAPTERS and VIDEO DISCUSSIONS WITH DAN KENNEDY AND KRISTI FRANK FROM *THE APPRENTICE* AVAILABLE AT:

www.NoBSBooks.com

Other Titles

THE ULTIMATE SALES LETTER (Adams Media)

THE ULTIMATE MARKETING PLAN (Adams Media)

How to Make Millions with Your Ideas (Plume/Penguin)

NO RULES: 21 Giant Lies about Success (Plume/Penguin)

The NEW Psycho-Cybernetics w. Maxwell Maltz, MD (PH Press)

My Unfinished Business/Autobiographical Essays (www.RenegadeMillionaire.com)

Index